Student Support Materials for AQA

AS/A-level Year 1

Biology

Topics 3 and 4: Organisms exchange substances with their environment, Genetic information, variation and relationships between organisms

Author: Mike Boyle

William Collins' dream of knowledge for all began with the publication of his first book in 1819. A self-educated mill worker, he not only enriched millions of lives, but also founded a flourishing publishing house. Today, staying true to this spirit, Collins books are packed with inspiration, innovation and practical expertise. They place you at the centre of a world of possibility and give you exactly what you need to explore it.

Collins. Freedom to teach

HarperCollins Publishers
The News Building
1 London Bridge Street
London SE1 9GF

Browse the complete Collins catalogue at
www.collins.co.uk

10 9 8 7 6 5 4 3 2 1

© HarperCollins*Publishers* 2016

ISBN 978-0-00-818946-4

Collins® is a registered trademark of HarperCollins*Publishers* Limited

www.collins.co.uk

A catalogue record for this book is available from the British Library

Commissioned by Gillian Lindsey
Edited by Alexander Rutherford
Project managed by Maheswari PonSaravanan at Jouve
Development by Kate Redmond and Gillian Lindsey
Copyedited by Rebecca Ramsden
Proofread by Janette Schubert
Original design by Newgen Imaging
Typeset by Jouve India Private Limited
Cover design by Angela English
Printed by CPI Group (UK) Ltd, Croydon, CR0 4YY
Cover image © iStock/royaltystockphoto

HarperCollins does not warrant that www.collins.co.uk or any other website mentioned in this title will be provided uninterrupted, that any website will be error free, that defects will be corrected, or that the website or the server that makes it available are free of viruses or bugs. For full terms and conditions please refer to the site terms provided on the website.

Contents

3.3 Organisms exchange substances with their environment

3.3.1 Surface area to volume ratio

The size and surface area problem

All organisms need to exchange materials with their surroundings. They need to exchange respiratory gases (carbon dioxide and oxygen), take in food and get rid of waste. The quantity of materials that an organism *needs* to exchange varies according to its *volume* – the amount of living tissue it has.

However, the quantity of material that an organism is *able to exchange* is proportional to its surface area. *As organisms get larger, the surface area : volume ratio decreases.* (See Table 1). For larger organisms, this effect is a problem. It makes it increasingly difficult to exchange both materials and heat with the environment fast enough to keep conditions inside the organism constant.

Table 1
Surface area and volume of a cube

Length of side/mm	Surface area/mm^2	Volume/mm^3	Surface area : volume ratio
1	6	1	6
2	24	8	3
3	54	27	2
10	600	1000	0.6

Surface area, heat and metabolic rate

The control of body temperature is known as **thermoregulation**. Mammals and birds can maintain a constant core body temperature using their physiology and their behaviour.

All other animals are, to a large extent, at the mercy of the environment. They can gain or lose heat by their behaviour, for example, crocodiles gape to keep cool, and many reptiles bask in the sun to warm up. However, their body temperature generally reflects that of their surroundings. These organisms are said to be ectothermic because their body heat comes mainly from outside their body.

Mammals and birds produce heat as a by-product of metabolism, and thermoregulate by controlling its loss into the environment. The amount of heat an organism can make depends on two things:

- Its volume, in other words, the mass of living tissue that it has
- Its **metabolic rate**, the number and speed of chemical reactions going on in its cells.

Metabolic rate can be measured by the amount of oxygen the animal uses (volume of oxygen per unit body weight per unit time) or by the amount of heat it produces (kJ of energy per unit body weight per unit time).

A large animal, such as an elephant or a hippopotamus, has a huge amount of heat-producing tissue and a relatively small surface area through which to lose it. Such an animal needs strategies to lose heat. These can include:

- Physical adaptations – large ears with a good blood supply near to the surface, to lose heat from the blood
- Behavioural adaptations – increasing evaporation of water from the body surface by mud and water bathing
- Physiological adaptations – having a relatively low metabolic rate.

Small animals, such as shrews, have the opposite problem. Their surface area to volume ratio is so large that the animal must have a very high metabolic rate to keep warm. Shrews have to eat constantly so that they have enough fuel to respire and generate body heat.

> **Notes**
> A common mistake is to say that a large animal has a small surface area. An elephant has a very large surface area, but it has a small surface area to volume ratio.

3.3.2 Gas exchange

Why do organisms need to exchange gases?

There are three main reasons:

- Most organisms take in oxygen and release carbon dioxide during aerobic **respiration**.
- In anaerobic conditions, some organisms, such as yeast and bacteria, release carbon dioxide without absorbing oxygen.
- Plants take in carbon dioxide and release oxygen when photosynthesis exceeds the rate of aerobic respiration.

Gas exchange occurs by diffusion, and gas exchange organs all show the same basic adaptations that maximise diffusion:

- a large surface area
- thin membranes, so the distance for diffusion is as short as possible
- an efficient transport system, which maintains a diffusion gradient.

Gas exchange in single-celled organisms

Single-celled organisms include bacteria and several different types of **protoctist**, including algae and amoeba. Being small, they have a large surface area to volume ratio, so the exchange of materials is no problem. Exchange takes place over the whole surface of the organism. However, for organisms to become larger (more than about 1 mm^3) they must become multicellular, and have some way of increasing the surface area for exchange of materials and heat.

Some multicellular organisms are elongated, flat or hollow, such as sea anemones and tapeworms, which are both invertebrates. In these organisms, materials exchanged between the cells and the environment have only a short distance to diffuse.

> **Notes**
> Gas exchange always occurs by **diffusion** alone. Not facilitated diffusion, not active transport, not osmosis.

More complex multicellular organisms have evolved specialist gas exchange organs such as lungs. Three more gas exchange solutions are studied here: gas exchange in insects, fish and plants.

Gas exchange in insects

Insects solve the gas exchange problem in a unique way. They have a **tracheal system** that consists of a network of tubes that branch out and take air directly from the outside and into the respiring tissues (Fig 1).

Fig 1
The tracheal system in insects. Air enters tiny tracheoles that pass very close to each respiring cell. The distances involved are so short that diffusion is rapid and efficient enough to meet the insect's needs.

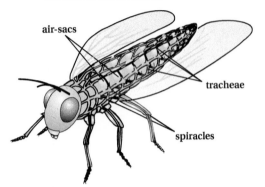

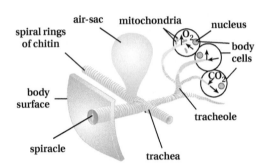

Air enters through holes in the insect's exoskeleton called **spiracles**. It then passes into tubes called **tracheae** (sing. trachea), which branch out into smaller **tracheoles**. The key difference between these two types of tube is that tracheae have thicker supportive walls whereas tracheoles have thin permeable walls that allow gas exchange.

The tracheoles form a fine network of tubes that pass within a short diffusing distance of all the respiring cells in the insect's body. Some tracheoles actually enter the cells, delivering oxygen directly to the mitochondria.

Essential Notes

Compared to lungs and gills, this may seem a strange way to breathe air, but diffusion of O_2 and CO_2 through air is very rapid, making the insect's system very efficient. However, it doesn't work in large organisms – this is one reason why insects are limited in size.

Insects can open or close their spiracles to alter the level of ventilation, and to minimise water loss. Some insects with a high metabolic rate are able to increase ventilation by contracting the muscles of their abdomen.

Gas exchange in fish

The gills of a fish are adapted for gas exchange in water, which is much denser than air but contains less available oxygen making it harder to extract a large volume of oxygen from water than from air. Animals that breathe in water are all cold blooded ectotherms and have a lower oxygen demand than mammals or birds.

Air versus water as a breathing medium

Air and water have very different properties and require completely different gas exchange systems:

- Air contains about 20% oxygen compared with around 1% or less for water.

- The oxygen content of air is very stable, whereas the oxygen content of water can vary considerably. The warmer the water, the lower the amount of dissolved oxygen it can hold.

- Diffusion of gases is much faster through air than through water. As a consequence, diffusion is rapid through the tracheoles of insects and the air sacs of mammalian lungs. However, it is slow where it has to pass through the liquid lining the alveoli and, of course, in fish gills.

- Water is much denser than air, so it takes much more effort to move it around. Air-breathing animals can inhale, reverse the direction of flow and breathe out with comparatively little effort. It would not be possible to do this with large volumes of water, so aquatic organisms let water flow over their gills in one direction only.

Gas exchange in the fish gill

The essential gas exchange features of a gill are:

- The **gill lamellae** and **gill filaments** have a large surface area (Fig 2).

- The **counter-current system** facilitates gas exchange (Fig 3).

The numerous gill filaments, and even more numerous lamellae, have a rich blood supply. Their thin membranes allow blood to come very close to the water. The blood in the capillaries flows in the opposite direction to the way water flows over the gills, which is why this is known as a counter-current system.

If the blood and water flowed in the same direction, oxygen would diffuse into the blood until an equilibrium was reached, at which point there would be no further net gas exchange. At any point along the filament in a counter-current system, the blood always has a lower concentration of oxygen than the water next to it (see Fig 3). So, a diffusion gradient is maintained along the entire length of the filament. This ensures that oxygen can diffuse into the blood at every point along the filament and that the blood leaving the filament has a high concentration of oxygen.

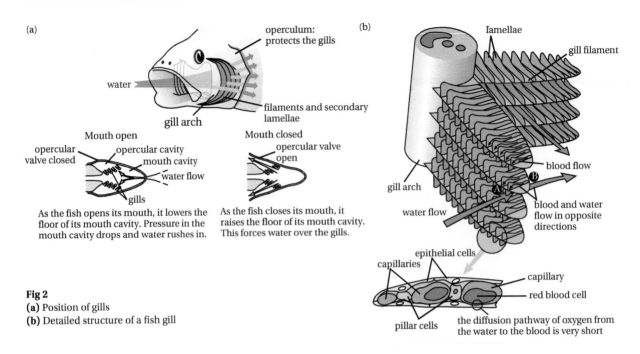

Fig 2
(a) Position of gills
(b) Detailed structure of a fish gill

the diffusion pathway of oxygen from the water to the blood is very short

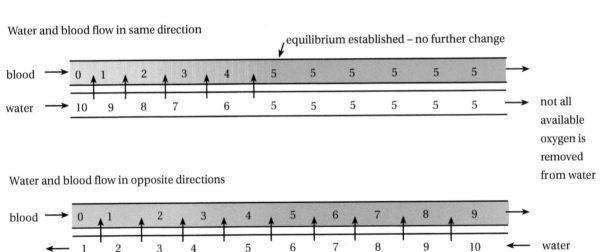

Fig 3
Diagram showing the importance of the counter-current system. The numbers refer to relative concentrations of dissolved oxygen. When blood flows in the opposite direction to the water, it continues to pass water that contains a higher concentration of oxygen. Thus the counter-current system allows the blood to absorb much more oxygen.

Gas exchange in plants

The leaf is an organ adapted to maximise photosynthesis. As photosynthesis requires carbon dioxide and produces oxygen, the leaf must be an efficient gas exchange structure. The palisade cells carry out most of the photosynthesis, and so the structure of the leaf centres around giving the palisade cells what they need (light, carbon dioxide and water) and taking away what they produce (sugar and oxygen). A section through the leaf (Fig 4) shows the following adaptations:

- Loosely packed **mesophyll** cells. This means there are air spaces between cells, providing a large cell surface area for gas exchange.

- **Stomata** open to allow gases to diffuse in and out of the internal air spaces along their concentration gradients (the stomata close at night to reduce water loss).

These adaptations mean that the cells that carry out the most photosynthesis are in direct contact with the environment.

Essential Notes

The syllabus specifies a dicotyledonous plant, or dicot, which generally means a 'standard' flowering plant. There are two main types of flowering plants: the monocotyledons, for example, the grasses, and the **dicotyledons**, which include most other familiar flowering plant species.

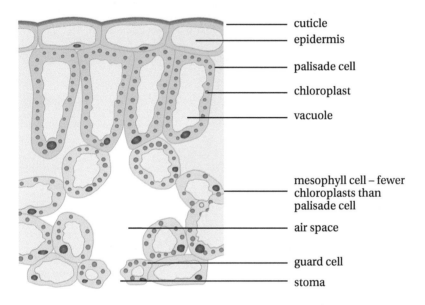

cuticle
epidermis
palisade cell
chloroplast
vacuole

mesophyll cell – fewer chloroplasts than palisade cell

air space

guard cell
stoma

Fig 4
A section through the leaf of a dicotyledonous plant

Water loss is an inevitable consequence of gas exchange with air. Gas exchange organs must have a large surface area and must also be permeable, so water loss by evaporation cannot be avoided. Dry air has a very low water potential, but humid air has a higher one. Evaporation takes place whenever there is a water potential gradient. In both insects and plants, gas exchange results in pockets of humid air called diffusion shells, which develop around spiracles or stomata. Protecting theses diffusion shells will minimise water loss.

Terrestrial (land-living) insects minimise water loss by:

- Closing their spiracles when not active
- Having hairs around the spiracle to minimise air movements, so that the humid air is not blown away
- The exoskeleton itself is made from waterproof chitin.

Similarly, **xerophytic** plants can minimise water loss by

- Reducing the number of stomata
- Having stomata in pits

- Having hairs around the stomata
- A thicker cuticle
- Rolling the leaf so the stomata are protected on the inside
- Reducing the surface area of leaves. Cacti take this to the extreme, where the leaves are reduced to spines and the stem becomes the main site of photosynthesis.

Gas exchange in humans

The basic structure of the lungs is shown in Fig 5 and the bronchial tree is shown in Fig 6.

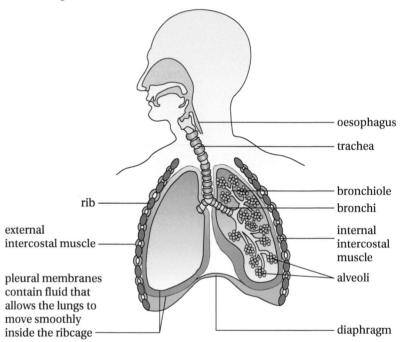

Fig 5
Basic structure of the lungs

Fig 6
The bronchial tree. Note that the terminal bronchioles are made from smooth muscle and not supported by cartilage. Asthma is caused by a contraction in the smooth muscle, obstructing the passage of air in and out of the alveoli. In particular, it is difficult to breathe out. That's what causes the wheezing sound.

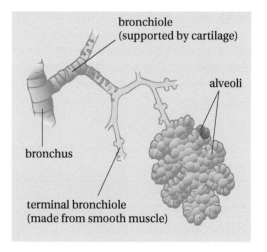

Breathing in humans

Lungs have two basic functions:

- They get as much air as possible into close contact with blood. They do this by having millions of tiny air sacs – **alveoli** – surrounded by a dense network of blood capillaries (Fig 7).

- They **ventilate** the gas exchange surfaces – the alveoli – so they have a constant supply of fresh air with high oxygen and low carbon dioxide concentration.

Single alveolus

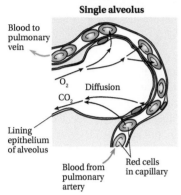

Each alveolus is a tiny air sac that has thin, flat walls. Oxygen from the air dissolves in the liquid that lines the alveolus and then diffuses across into the blood capillary. Carbon dioxide leaves the blood by the reverse route.

Fig 7
Alveoli with capillary showing the short distance over which oxygen and carbon dioxide have to diffuse

Notes

The alveolar wall is made from thin, flat cells classified as **simple squamous epithelium**. The **alveolar epithelium** aids rapid diffusion by presenting as thin a barrier as possible between blood and air.

Air that enters the lungs passes down the bronchial tree through large tubes (**trachea, bronchi**) into progressively smaller ones (first **bronchioles**, then **terminal bronchioles**) and finally into the alveoli. Gas exchange takes place across the alveolar walls and the capillary walls.

Definition

Ventilation is the act of pumping fresh air in and out of the lungs, over the gas exchange surfaces, so that a diffusion gradient is maintained.

The mechanism of ventilation

Mammalian lungs contain no muscle, so cannot move on their own. Ventilation is brought about by the **intercostal** muscles and the **diaphragm**. The intercostal muscles are found between the ribs. There are two types: internal intercostal muscles and external intercostal muscles. These two types of muscle have an **antagonistic** interaction – when the internal intercostal muscles contract, the external muscles relax, and vice versa.

This is what happens when we breathe in:

- Nerve impulses pass down nerves from the **respiratory centre** in the **medulla** of the brain to the intercostal muscles and the diaphragm.

- The internal intercostal muscles relax while the external intercostal muscles contract. This pulls the ribs up and out while the diaphragm flattens, pushing the abdominal organs downwards.

- The volume of the thorax increases, lowering the pressure below that of the atmosphere, so air is forced into the lungs.

Notes

Beware of statements like 'alveolar cells have thin membranes' because they do not. A membrane is a general word for a barrier, and this causes confusion. Alveolar cells have cell membranes that are the same thickness as all other cell membranes. However, the alveolar cells are thin and flat, so that the epithelial cells themselves form a thin membrane.

Essential Notes

You should be able to change the subject of this equation, for example to find the tidal volume if you are given values for pulmonary ventilation rate and breathing rate.

Notes

Remember that when volume increases, pressure decreases and vice versa.

Definitions

Breathing: some key definitions

Tidal volume = *the volume of air inhaled/exhaled in each breath.* 500 cm³ *is an average value for human tidal volume while at rest.*

Breathing rate = *the number of breaths in one minute.* 14 *would be an average value while at rest.*

Pulmonary ventilation rate = **Tidal volume × breathing rate**

Using the above values we get a value for pulmonary ventilation rate of 7000 cm³ *per minute or, more simply,* 7 litres per minute.

Breathing out is largely a *passive* process – it does not require muscular contraction unless we want to speed up the process. Elastic recoil of the abdominal muscles, along with the weight of the ribcage and pressure of abdominal organs, decreases the volume of the thorax. This, together with the natural elastic recoil of the lung tissue, increases pressure inside the lungs and air is forced out through the bronchial system. To forcibly exhale, we use our internal intercostal muscles, helped by the abdominal muscles which force the diaphragm upwards.

Effect of lung disease on gas exchange and ventilation

Examiners may use questions on lung diseases as an opportunity to test your understanding of normal lung function.

Fibrosis

Fibrosis is a process by which normal tissues of an organ suffer damage and are replaced by fibrous connective tissue: 'scar tissue'. The delicate alveoli of the lungs are particularly vulnerable to fibrosis. Widespread fibrosis due to smoking or other air pollution is called emphysema, while tuberculosis can leave small patches of fibrosis caused by bacterial infection. Thus, fibrosis is a consequence of disease rather than a disease in its own right.

Tuberculosis (TB)

TB is a bacterial disease of the lungs caused by two species: *Mycobacterium tuberculosis* and *Mycobacterium bovis*. Symptoms include a persistent cough, blood-smeared sputum, shortness of breath, fever and, in the long term, weight loss.

In a person with a healthy immune system, the presence of the bacteria stimulates a response that attempts to stop the bacteria from spreading. Patches of infection become surrounded by white cells and then scar tissue, which isolates the bacteria, preventing them from spreading to other parts of the lung. This scar tissue is detectable by radiography and shows up as dark shadows on an X-ray.

In the long term, therefore, TB leaves the individual with patches of fibrosis, which reduces the overall surface area for gas exchange.

Emphysema

Emphysema is permanent lung damage (see 'fibrosis' above) caused by smoking and air pollutants. The delicate alveolar walls become damaged and replaced with connective tissue. The result is twofold:

* There is a loss of surface area and a thickening of the alveolar walls, making gas exchange less efficient (Fig 8).

Fig 8
Healthy alveoli above compared to an individual with emphysema below. Note the decrease in surface area and the thicker walls – classic symptoms of emphysema.

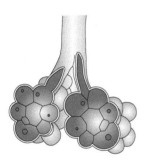

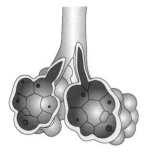

- There is a loss of *elasticity*. Normal lungs are elastic and will exhale of their own accord, with very little muscular effort needed from the lungs or diaphragm. Emphysemic patients have to make more of an effort to breathe out.

The main cause is smoking – 80% of cases of emphysema occur in people who smoke. Emphysema usually affects older people as it is due to cumulative damage over a long period, such as a lifetime of smoking.

Asthma

Asthma is the most common lung disease, affecting an estimated 5.2 million people in the UK alone. Asthma is a difficulty in breathing caused by a **constriction** of the smooth muscle that makes up the terminal bronchioles (see Fig 6). The muscular walls swell and secrete more mucus than normal.

During an asthma attack the flow of air is reduced, so ventilation is less efficient. The actual surface area of the alveoli is unchanged, and people can recover from asthma with no damage to the lungs whatsoever. Asthma is not like TB and emphysema, where fibrosis occurs.

> **Notes**
> Many exam questions contain data about risk factors and ask you to interpret them. You also need to be able to interpret data on correlations.

3.3.3 Digestion and absorption

This section is about what is in food and how we digest it. First, some basics:

- The food we eat contains plant and animal tissue, which contains lots of large, complex molecules locked inside cells.

- Food also contains some bacteria, which may or may not be harmful.

- In **digestion**, we must first break open the cells – cooking and chewing food both help. We then **hydrolyse** (break down the compound by reacting with water) the large molecules until they are small enough to be absorbed into the blood.

- The main types of large organic molecules are **protein**, **carbohydrate** and **lipid**.

- Proteins are hydrolysed into **amino acids**.

- Carbohydrates are hydrolysed into **simple sugars**, mainly **glucose**.

- Lipids are hydrolysed into **fatty acids** and **glycerol**.

- These molecules, along with minerals, vitamins and water, are absorbed into the blood through the gut wall (mainly in the small intestine).

- Once inside the body the simple food molecules are assimilated; they are used to make cells and cell components, or broken down for energy.

Overview of the digestive system

The human gut is essentially a long, muscular tube that stretches from mouth to anus.

Various glands along the gut secrete digestive juices. There are four main digestive juices:

- **Saliva**: made by three pairs of salivary glands in the mouth.

- **Gastric juice**: made by the stomach lining.

- **Bile**: secreted by the liver.

- **Pancreatic juice**: made by the pancreas.

These juices contain a variety of substances that control the digestive process.

Generally, these four main digestive juices begin digestion but the process is finished off by enzymes fixed in the membrane of the epithelial cells in the gut lining.

Carbohydrate digestion

Polysaccharides and **disaccharides** must be digested to **monosaccharides** before they can be absorbed.

Carbohydrate digestion begins in the mouth when the **amylase** enzyme in saliva begins to hydrolyse starch into maltose. This is only partial breakdown at best, because food doesn't stay in the mouth for long, and hot food can denature the enzyme. The acidic conditions in the stomach also deactivate salivary amylase.

There is no significant carbohydrate digestion in the stomach. Most carbohydrate digestion takes place in the duodenum. First, pancreatic amylase hydrolyses starch into maltose. Then carbohydrate digestion is completed by enzymes fixed in the membranes of the epithelial cells. The three vital **membrane-bound disaccharidases** are maltase, lactase and sucrase:

- Maltase hydrolyses maltose into two molecules of glucose.
- Lactase hydrolyses lactose into a glucose and a galactose.
- Sucrase hydrolyses sucrose into a glucose and a fructose.

Lipid digestion

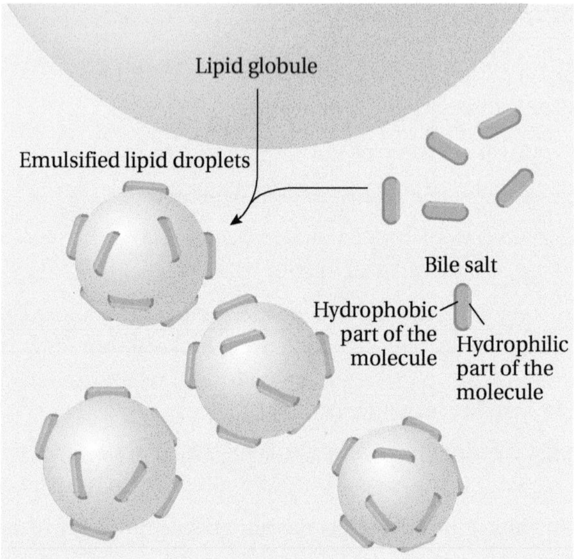

Essential Notes

Amylases remove disaccharides from the end of polysaccharide chains. This is why starch is hydrolysed to maltose.

Fig 9
How bile salts help lipids disperse in water

There is no significant digestion of lipid until the small intestine. There are two aspects to lipid digestion: physical and chemical.

Physical digestion is done by **bile**, which is a greenish fluid, made in the liver, stored in the gall bladder and delivered to the intestine via the bile duct. Bile contains no enzymes, but does contain **bile salts**. Lipids are non-polar molecules and so do not mix with water. Lipids in the gut form large droplets. Bile salts have both polar and non-polar regions to their molecules, and so are part **hydrophilic** and part **hydrophobic**. As a consequence, bile salts interact with both lipid and water, lowering the surface tension between them and resulting in smaller droplets called **micelles**, which have a much larger surface area than the original lipid droplets. **Lipase** enzymes can act on the surface of the micelles.

Pancreatic lipase, present in pancreatic juice, breaks down triglycerides by **hydrolysis** of some or all of the ester bonds. This results in a mixture of three compounds: glycerol, fatty acids and monoglycerides (glycerol which is still joined to one fatty acid). These molecules also form part of the micelles, with their hydrophilic parts facing outwards towards the water.

Protein digestion

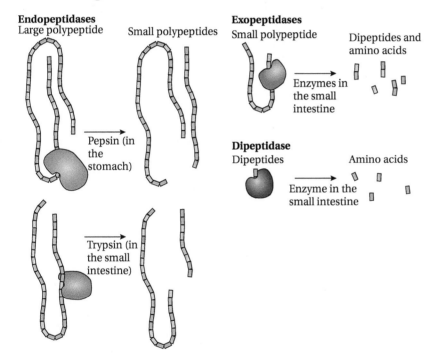

Endopeptidases
Large polypeptide   Small polypeptides

Pepsin (in the stomach)

Trypsin (in the small intestine)

Exopeptidases
Small polypeptide   Dipeptides and amino acids

Enzymes in the small intestine

Dipeptidase
Dipeptides   Amino acids

Enzyme in the small intestine

Fig 10
Protein-digesting enzymes in the alimentary canal

Protein digestion starts in the stomach and is completed in the small intestine. Generally, there are two types of **protease** enzymes.

1 Endopeptidases – enzymes that cut polypeptides *within* the chain, turning long polypeptides into shorter ones. This digestion does not produce individual amino acids.

2 Exopeptidases – enzymes that remove the terminal (end) amino acids from the chain.

These two enzyme types work very effectively together – 'synergistically' – their combined effect is greater than the sum of their individual contributions. This is because the endopeptidases provide more ends for the exopeptidases to work on.

Protein digestion region by region

In the stomach gastric glands in the gastric mucosa (stomach lining) secrete gastric juice which contains the enzyme **pepsin**, an endopeptidase.

In the small intestine pancreatic juice is added to food. This contains the endopeptidase **trypsin**. This is a different endopeptidase to pepsin and so will cut different **peptide bonds**, thus making even smaller polypeptides.

Protein digestion is completed by **exopeptidases** which are embedded in the membranes of the epithelial cells that line the gut. The action of these enzymes results in individual amino acids.

Absorption

Proteins can only be absorbed as amino acids, which are absorbed in the same way as glucose: **co-transport** (see Fig 11).

Glycerol, fatty acids and monoglycerides break off the micelles and pass into the epithelial cells, where they enter the endoplasmic reticulum. Note that the micelles themselves are not absorbed.

The glycerol, fatty acids and monoglycerides are re-formed into triglycerides in the endoplasmic reticulum of the epithelial cells. Along with protein, phospholipids and cholesterol, they form droplets called **chylomicrons**. The hydrophilic molecules in the mixture (phospholipid heads and proteins) make chylomicrons soluble in water, and this allows triglycerides to be transported in blood plasma. The chylomicrons leave the epithelial cells by exocytosis, where they enter the **lacteals** (lymph capillaries). The chylomicrons travel in the lymph system until they drain into the blood system in the upper thorax.

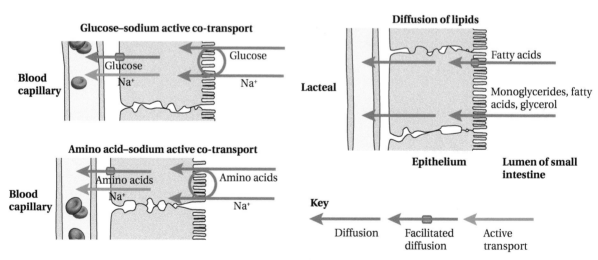

Fig 11
Absorption across the intestinal epithelium

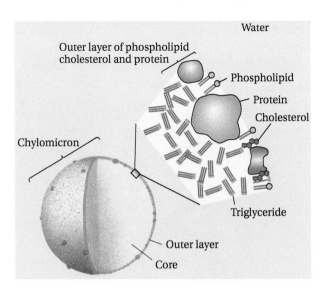

Fig 12
A chylomicron

3.3.4 Mass transport

There are many different organs of gas exchange such as lungs and gills, but these organs would be ineffective without a distribution network to the rest of the body. To be effective, gas exchange organs need a circulatory system, which usually takes the form of a network of tubes or vessels that connects to all parts of the organism.

Many organisms have **vascular systems** (vascular = tube/vessel). Plants have xylem and phloem while many animals have a circulatory blood system. The movement of large volumes of fluid and dissolved substances within a transport system is known as **mass flow**.

3.3.4.1 Mass transport in animals
Haemoglobin (Hb)

Haemoglobin is a vital protein:

- It occurs in red blood cells (Fig 13), where it has a vital role in oxygen transport.

- It is a protein with a **quaternary structure** because it is made from four **polypeptide** chains (Fig 14).

- It has the remarkable ability to pick up oxygen where it is abundant (the lungs) and release it where it is needed (the respiring **tissues**).

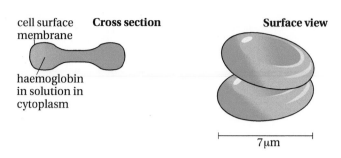

Fig 13
Red blood cells. The biconcave shape of the red cell is an efficient compromise between the maximum volume of a sphere and the maximum surface area of a flat disc. This allows the cells to carry a useful amount of oxygen, but to load and unload it quickly.

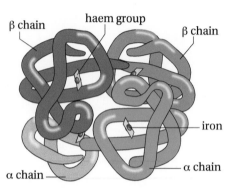

Fig 14
The haemoglobin molecule consists of 4 polypeptide chains, two α globins and two β globins. Each chain is attached to a haem group featuring a central iron (Fe^{2+}) ion that combines with an oxygen molecule.

Oxygen is carried mainly as oxyhaemoglobin in the red blood cells. As the equation below shows, each haemoglobin molecule can combine with four oxygen molecules:

Hb	+	$4O_2$	HbO_8
haemoglobin		oxygen	oxyhaemoglobin

A key point about haemoglobin is not that it can pick up oxygen – lots of substances can do that – but that it can release it again in areas where it is needed. The behaviour of haemoglobin with oxygen is illustrated by the **oxygen dissociation curve** (Fig 15).

There are two key features of the oxygen dissociation curve.

1   At the high oxygen concentrations found in the lungs, where the curve is level, haemoglobin becomes almost fully saturated with oxygen.

2   At the low oxygen concentration found in the tissues, where the curve is steep, oxyhaemoglobin dissociates, releasing much of its oxygen. In this part of the curve, a small drop in oxygen concentration can cause a relatively large change in the percentage saturation of the haemoglobin, which releases large amounts of oxygen.

At a higher concentration of carbon dioxide, the curve is shifted to the right. This is because carbon dioxide is an acidic gas that *lowers the* **affinity** *of haemoglobin for oxygen*. This is known as the **Bohr effect**. The significance of this is seen in metabolically active tissues, such as muscles; the harder they are working, the more carbon dioxide they produce and the more oxygen is released by the haemoglobin.

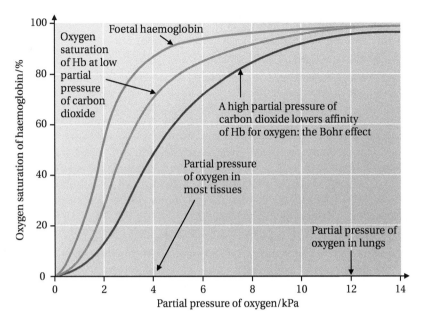

Fig 15
The oxygen dissociation curve and the Bohr effect.

Notes

The key idea with this graph is that the affinity of haemoglobin for oxygen can change. The more carbon dioxide there is, the lower the affinity of haemoglobin for oxygen.

Notes

Questions featuring this graph are likely to involve a calculation about oxygen transfer. Make sure that you can use the oxygen dissociation curve to predict a change in the percentage saturation of haemoglobin. An exam question could ask you, for example, to predict the change when the partial pressure changes from 4 kPa to 12 kPa. For the foetal curve, for example, it would be 18% (98% at 12 minus 80% at 12).

The steps involved in the release of oxygen at the tissues are shown in Fig 16 and listed below:

1   Carbon dioxide diffuses out of the respiring cell, through the **plasma** and into the red blood cell.

2   The enzyme **carbonic anhydrase** catalyses the reaction between carbon dioxide and water, speeding up the production of carbonic acid, which dissociates into H^+ ions and HCO_3^- (hydrogen carbonate) ions.

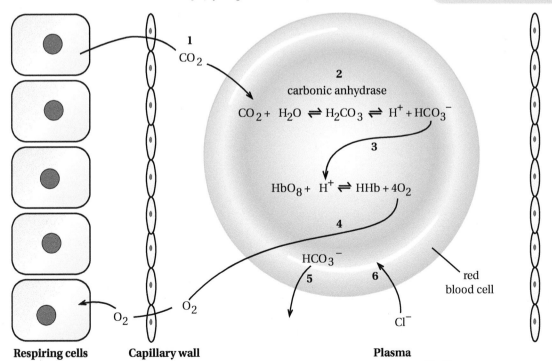

Fig 16
Steps in the release of oxygen at the tissues.

Notes

It is important to distinguish between the production of HCO_3^- in the red cells, and the transport of HCO_3^- in the plasma.

3   The H^+ ions combine with haemoglobin, causing the release of the oxygen.

4   The free oxygen molecules diffuse into the respiring cells.

5   The HCO_3^- ions diffuse into the plasma. This causes the red cell to develop a slight positive charge. To counteract this, Cl^- ions flow into the red cell. This is known as the chloride shift.

Most carbon dioxide is transported as HCO_3^- in the plasma.

Haemoglobin across the animal kingdom

Many aquatic invertebrates also make use of haemoglobin. There is much less oxygen in water than in air, and the warmer the water, the less oxygen it can hold. In polluted water oxygen can be especially scarce because the bacteria also compete for what little there is. The following species all owe their red colouration to the presence of haemoglobin.

●   Tubifex worms live in poorly oxygenated mud at the bottom of rivers and ponds. They burrow head first into the mud, leaving their tails sticking out. The oxygen dissociation curve for tubifex worms is shown in Fig 17.

●   Chironomid midge larvae (bloodworms) live in burrows, also in poorly oxygenated mud. They must come out from time to time to replenish their oxygen stores. The haemoglobin in their tissues allows them to store oxygen and stay in the burrow for longer, thus avoiding predators.

Fig 17
The oxygen dissociation curve for haemoglobin from the tubifex worm lies to the left of the curve for human haemoglobin. This shows that tubifex haemoglobin has a higher affinity for oxygen than human haemoglobin.

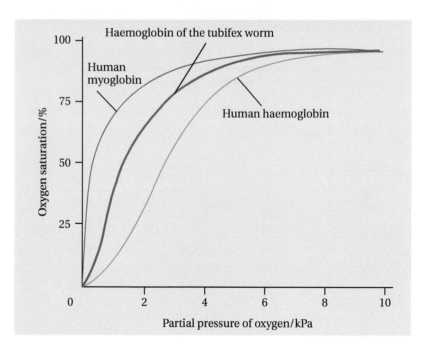

Notes

In questions involving this graph, examiners expect so see the correct terminology, so words such as **affinity, saturation** and **partial pressure** should be used.

Heart structure and function

Mammals have a double circulation; a **pulmonary circulation** and a **systemic circulation**.

The pulmonary circulation takes blood on the relatively short return journey to the lungs, where blood is oxygenated. When blood passes through a system of capillaries it loses pressure, so it must return to the heart for a pressure boost before it enters the systemic circulation, which takes blood around the rest of the body.

(a)

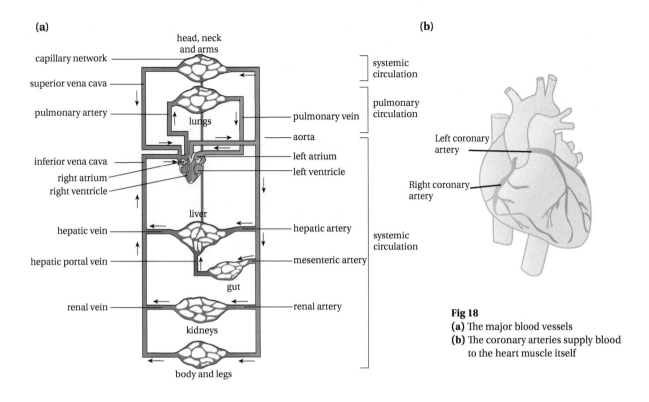

(b)

Fig 18
(a) The major blood vessels
(b) The coronary arteries supply blood to the heart muscle itself

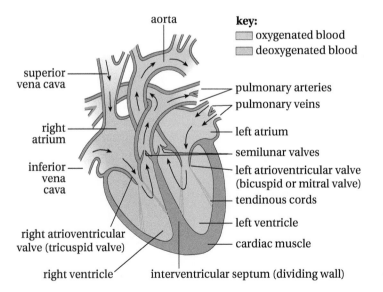

key:
- oxygenated blood
- deoxygenated blood

Fig 19
The structure of the heart

Notes

Make sure that you can label a section through the heart, including the chambers, valves and blood vessels.

The mammalian heart acts as the pump for both the pulmonary and the systemic systems. It has four chambers; two **atria** and two **ventricles** (Fig 19). All chambers have approximately the same volume, so with each heartbeat an equal volume of blood passes to the lungs and to the whole of the rest of the body. **Atrioventricular** (AV) **valves** prevent backflow of blood from ventricles to atria. **Semilunar valves** prevent backflow of blood from arteries into ventricles.

Cardiac output is the volume of blood pumped by the heart per minute. Each heartbeat is known as the **cardiac cycle**. This can be divided into three stages:

1 Both atria contract – the **atrial systole** – this takes about 0.1 seconds.

2 Both ventricles contract – the **ventricular systole** – this takes about 0.3 seconds.

3 All chambers relax – the **diastole** – this lasts about 0.4 seconds.

The regular beating of the heart is not under the control of the brain, although impulses from the brain modify the heart rate, making it faster or slower.

Fig 20
The events of the cardiac cycle – each numbered event is described in the text

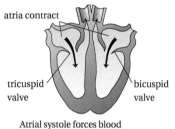

atria contract

tricuspid valve — bicuspid valve

Atrial systole forces blood into ventricles. AV valves open.

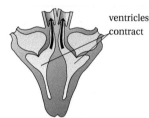

ventricles contract

Atria relax, ventricles contract, AV valves close, SL valves open. Blood goes into aorta and pulmonary artery.

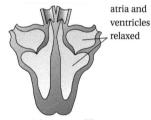

atria and ventricles relaxed

Atria begin to refill. Ventricles are in diastole.

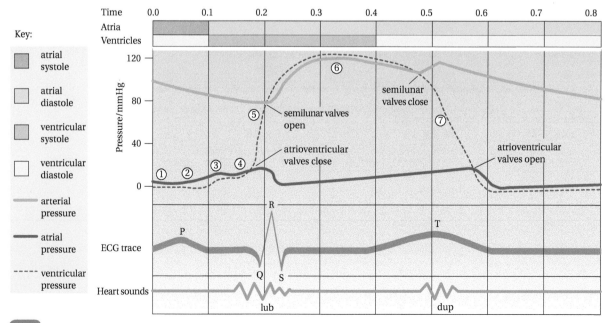

It is important to remember what is cause and what is effect in the heart. The electrical impulses initiate muscular contraction, the contraction squeezes the blood, increasing the pressure and forcing blood in a particular direction. This blood flow opens or closes valves. The valves are just tough flaps of tissue – they do not open and close on their own.

So, the cardiac cycle takes about 0.8 seconds in total, resulting in a heart rate of 75 beats per minute – about average for a young, resting person. The heart rate speeds up during exercise, and the safe maximum for humans is 220 beats per minute minus your age. Therefore, the maximum safe heart rate for a healthy 20-year-old would be 200.

The events of the cardiac cycle (Fig 20) can be summarised as follows:

1 Both atria fill with blood.

2 Both atria contract, causing the pressure in the atria to rise. When the pressure in the atria rises above that in the ventricles, blood is forced through the atrio-ventricular valves and so the ventricles fill.

3 After a short delay, the ventricles contract. As soon as the pressure in the ventricles exceeds that in the atria, the AV valves are forced shut (causing the first heart sound, 'dup'). At this point, all the valves are closed and the pressure in the ventricles rises dramatically.

4 When the pressure in the ventricles exceeds that in the aorta and pulmonary artery, blood is forced through the semi-lunar valves.

5 As soon as the ventricles start to relax, the pressure falls below that in the aorta and pulmonary arteries and so the semi-lunar valves close again (causing the second heart sound, 'dup').

Meanwhile, the atria fill with blood again and the cycle repeats itself.

Risk factors in the development of heart disease

Cardiovascular disease is the biggest single cause of death in the UK. It accounts for over a quarter of all deaths – about 175 000 per year. The common underlying cause of cardiovascular disease is a build-up of a fatty material, called atheroma, in the walls of arteries.

The build-up of atheroma is a process called **atherosclerosis**, and is usually the result of a combination of risk factors, both environmental and genetic.

Diet and blood cholesterol
Cholesterol is a perfectly natural substance, all cells contain some cholesterol and some cells have quite a lot. So it's not a deadly poison, it's important. These are the essential facts about cholesterol:

- Your body can make its own cholesterol, but it's also found in lots of the foods we eat.

- Eggs, cream and fatty meat are especially high in cholesterol. Note that these are all *animal products* – there's very little cholesterol in plants.

- High levels of cholesterol in the blood lead to a build-up of atheroma.

- Some unlucky people have a high level of cholesterol – it's genetic. These people have to watch what they eat.

Notes

You must be able to interpret graphs such as the one in Fig 20 without the labels. You should be able to label the points at which the valves open and close. For instance, the semilunar valves open when the pressure in the ventricles exceeds the pressure in the arteries.

Smoking

There is a well-established link between smoking and atherosclerosis, although the exact mechanism is complex. Certain substances in tobacco smoke constrict arteries, raising blood pressure.

High blood pressure

High blood pressure or hypertension can be the result of several factors: high salt intake, smoking, obesity and a genetic tendency.

Blood vessels

The structure and function of arteries, arterioles, veins and capillaries are summarised in Table 2 and their interrelationship is shown in Fig 21.

Fig 21
An overview of the different types of blood vessels

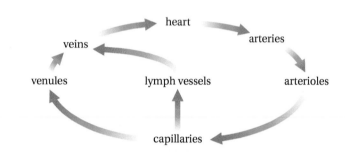

Table 2
Relating structure to function in blood vessel walls

Vessel	Diagram	Structure of wall	Function
Artery		Contains more elastic fibres than muscle; tough walls can withstand pressure surges as the heart beats.	Recoil; absorbs pressure when heart beats. Smooths out pulse wave. Maintains diastolic blood pressure.
Arteriole		Contains more muscle than elastic fibres; can **constrict** or **dilate**.	Controls blood supply to particular areas.
Capillary	endothelial cell	Thin, permeable.	Allows rapid diffusion and exchange.
Vein		Relatively thin; contains valves.	Prevents backflow.

Capillaries and tissue fluid

Tissue fluid surrounds all living cells. Cells obtain all their oxygen and nutrients from this fluid, swapping them for carbon dioxide and other wastes, such as urea. Its composition is similar to blood plasma, but without the large proteins. The function of capillaries is to allow the exchange of materials between tissue fluid and the blood (Fig 22).

Keeping the composition of tissue fluid constant is a major aspect of **homeostasis**. To understand how this is achieved we need to know two things:

- Why does tissue fluid form?

- Why does it drain away?

Two forces are important:

- **Hydrostatic pressure** – the fluid pressure of the blood, created by the left ventricle of the heart. This forces fluid out of the blood and into the tissues, forming tissue fluid.

- **Water potential** – this force, generated mainly by the proteins in the plasma, tends to draw fluid back into the blood by osmosis, which is why tissue fluid can drain away.

Tissue fluid is formed at the arterial end of a capillary because the hydrostatic pressure is greater than the water potential force. However, as fluid passes along the capillary it loses volume and, therefore, its pressure drops. When the hydrostatic pressure falls below the water potential, fluid drains back into the blood.

Arteries deliver all of the fluid to the tissues, but the veins do not drain all of it away. The lymphatic system drains away a small but vital proportion of tissue fluid. Lymph is similar to tissue fluid, but with more lipids and large proteins. This fluid passes into progressively larger lymph vessels, before draining into the blood system in the upper part of the chest cavity.

Notes

You may be given a section through a blood vessel and asked to identify it. You might also be asked to relate the structure of a vessel's wall to its function. Arteries have thick, elastic walls to cope with pressure. Arterioles have muscular walls so they can dilate or constrict. Veins are thin because they don't have to withstand high pressure, and the larger lumen minimises resistance to blood flow. Capillaries are thin and permeable to allow exchange between blood and surrounding tissues.

Notes

Revise water potential from Topic 3, section 3.2.3 to help you with this section. You must be able to express your examination answers in terms of water potential.

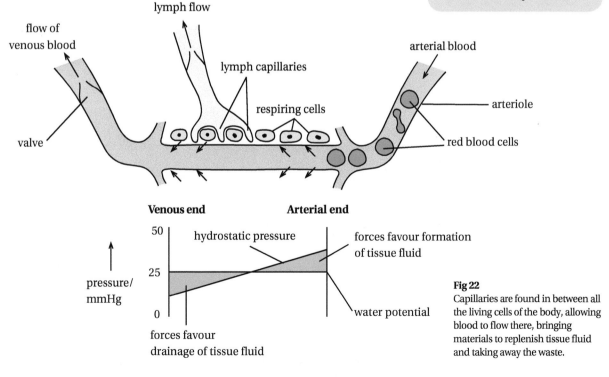

Fig 22
Capillaries are found in between all the living cells of the body, allowing blood to flow there, bringing materials to replenish tissue fluid and taking away the waste.

3.3.4.2 Mass transport in plants

Plants have specialised structures for transporting materials. The roots, stem and leaves form an organ system for transport of substances around the plant (Fig 23).

- **Xylem** – this tissue consists of many dead, hollow xylem vessels that carry water and dissolved mineral ions up the plant to the leaves and other organs.

- **Phloem** – this is tissue consisting mainly of living cells, which are tubular in shape. These cells are responsible for **translocation** in which dissolved organic materials, such as sucrose, are moved around the plant.

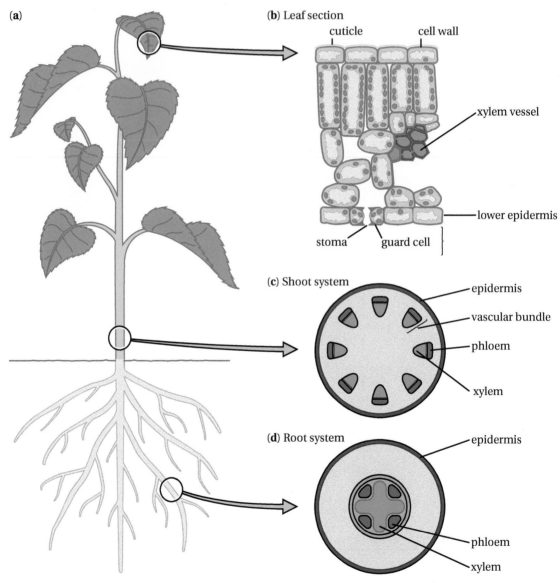

Fig 23
(a) Basic structure of a flowering plant
(b) Section through a leaf
(c) Section through a stem. Note the separate vascular bundles.
(d) Section through a root. Note the central vascular bundle and the x-shaped xylem.

Water uptake and the transpiration stream

You need to know two vital definitions:

Transpiration is the loss of water from the surfaces of a plant that are above the ground. Most water is lost through the **stomata** on the underside of leaves.

The **transpiration stream** is the continuous flow of water through the plant, from the roots to the leaves. The xylem tissue is mainly responsible for this flow.

Is water pushed or pulled up a plant?

The simple answer is; a bit of both. Two forces act to move water upwards:

- **Root pressure**, which pushes water up from beneath
- **Cohesion tension**, which pulls water up to the leaves.

Watching what happens when a stem is cut can demonstrate which is more important. If root pressure was greater, there would be a *positive* pressure in the stem – fluid would flow out of a cut stem. This sometimes happens, especially in small and younger plants, but usually there is a *negative* pressure inside the vessels of the stem showing that water is *pulled* up the plant. If a stem under negative pressure is cut, air is drawn in rather than fluid spurting out.

The cohesion–tension hypothesis

The main driving force of transpiration, which *pulls* water up the plant, is known as the cohesion-tension hypothesis. As water evaporates from the leaves, it creates a negative pressure in the xylem. This pulls a continuous column of water up from the roots. Water molecules are very cohesive; they stick together, forming a column with great tensile strength from the surface of the mesophyll cells (Fig 24), down the xylem to the roots.

The factors that raise the rate of transpiration are those that increase evaporation:

- **Temperature** – the higher the temperature, the faster water molecules evaporate
- **Humidity** – the amount of water vapour in the air. The more humid it is, the harder it is for water vapour to move out of the air spaces. The drier it is, the greater the **water potential gradient** between the air spaces and the atmosphere.
- **Air movement** – for example, wind speed. A breeze blows away the small pockets of humid air that develop around stomata when the air is still; humid air is replaced by drier air, so the water potential gradient is maintained.
- **Light** – this causes stomata to open, greatly increasing the passage of water vapour out of the plant.

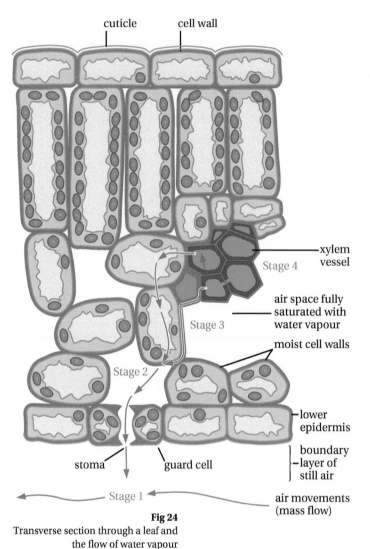

cuticle   cell wall

xylem vessel

Stage 4

air space fully saturated with water vapour

Stage 3

moist cell walls

Stage 2

lower epidermis

boundary layer of still air

stoma   guard cell

Stage 1   air movements (mass flow)

Fig 24
Transverse section through a leaf and
the flow of water vapour

Stage 1. Mass flow in air

Wind movements (mass flow) take air, fully saturated with water vapour, away from the leaf surface.

The air replacing it contains less water vapour and this maintains a concentration gradient for water vapour leaving the air spaces of a leaf.

Stage 2. Diffusion of water in still air

Water vapour diffuses down a concentration gradient through the leaf air spaces, through open stomata, and through the boundary layer of still air on the outside of the leaf.

Stage 3. Diffusion of water through cells

Water loss from the surface of cells lowers the water potential inside the cells.

Water at a higher potential diffuses from the nearest xylem vessel through leaf cells to replace the lost water.

Stage 4. Mass flow of water in xylem vessels

Pressure in xylem vessels is lowered as water leaves them.

Water moves up the xylem vessel from the roots where the pressure is higher.

Notes

The conditions that increase the speed of drying of clothes on a washing line – warm, dry, windy – also speed up transpiration.

Essential Notes

The circumference of a tree shows a measurable decrease when the plant is actively transpiring. The pull on the column of water actually makes the xylem vessels narrower. If the xylem vessels are pierced by a needle, however, air is drawn in, breaking the column and blocking the transpiration stream.

Measuring transpiration – the potometer

The **potometer** is a simple device for measuring the rate of transpiration from a cutting (Fig 25). Think of the glass tube as a transparent extension of the xylem.

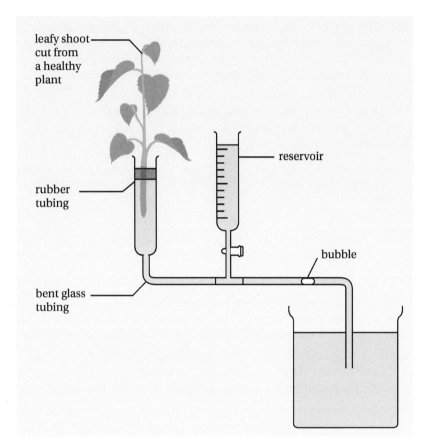

Fig 25
A potometer is a useful piece of apparatus for measuring the rate of transpiration from a cutting.

How it works:

- The shoot transpires.
- This results in water being drawn up the xylem.
- The bubble in the tube shows the rate of water uptake.
- The speed that the bubble moves is a measure of the rate of transpiration.

You can measure the volume of water being transpired in two ways:

1 By having the bubble in a calibrated tube of known volume.

2 By having a calibrated reservoir, and measuring the volume needed to move the bubble back to the start. This also allows the potometer to be re-started without having to dismantle all the apparatus.

The potometer can be used to measure the effect of various environmental conditions on the rate of transpiration. Light intensity, wind speed, relative humidity and temperature can all be investigated.

In practice, it is difficult to control all the variables. In particular, in order to get reliable data it is necessary to repeat the experiment using different shoots, and it is near impossible to get identical ones. They will differ in a variety of important ways, number and size of leaves, thickness of xylem tissue, number of stomata, water content of cells etc.

To compensate for the difference between shoots, it is necessary to calculate the surface area of each one. This is done by removing the leaves after the experiment and estimating their surface area by using squared paper. The units of transpiration are usually water loss per unit area per minute; $cm^3\ H_2O/m^2/min$.

Table 3 shows sample results from an investigation into the effect of air movement. For each trial, the water loss was measured every two minutes for 20 minutes.

Table 3
Sample results obtained using a potometer. Note that reading 4 has not been used in calculating the average for still air as it is an anomalous reading. While almost all biological data varies, an anomalous result is one that falls outside the normal range.

Trial number	Water loss/cm³ H₂O/m²/min					
	1	2	3	4	5	Average
Still air	2.4	2.8	3.1	0.6	2.5	2.7
Moving air	6.2	5.6	6.0	5.6	4.9	5.66

In order to get **valid** results the data needs to be **accurate**, **precise** and **repeatable**:

- Accurate results are close to the true value. Possible problems that will make the results inaccurate include a leaky seal between the shoot and the tube, incorrectly calibrated glassware or perhaps a fracture/break in the xylem tissue.

- Precise results depend on the nature of the apparatus being used. With a potometer calibrated in 0.1 ml intervals, it is plainly silly to have readings of 5.3428. Reading to one decimal place is precise enough in this situation.

- Repeatable data is obtained by doing repeats, so that all of the readings are close together. Any **anomalous results**, such as the 0.6 reading in trial 4, should not be included in the calculation of the mean.

The conclusion from these results, of course, is that plants transpire faster in windy conditions.

Translocation

Translocation is the movement of sucrose and other organic molecules in the **phloem** tissue, from **source** to **sink**.

The mass flow hypothesis

The **mass flow hypothesis** is a commonly used explanation for the mechanism of translocation. It explains why substances move up and down the plant, from source to sink.

1. Glucose is produced by photosynthesis at the source (the leaves) and converted into sucrose.

2. The sucrose is moved, by active transport, into the phloem.

3. The movement of sucrose lowers the **water potential** in the phloem.

4. Water enters the phloem from the **xylem** by osmosis, causing an increase in **hydrostatic pressure**.

5. Meanwhile, at the sink, the sucrose is absorbed from the phloem by active transport.

6. Water follows the sucrose, by osmosis.

7. The loss of water from the phloem lowers the hydrostatic pressure.

Overall, fluid in phloem is forced from the area of high hydrostatic pressure to the areas of lower hydrostatic pressure

Contrasting translocation with transpiration

- The driving force for transpiration is the evaporation of water from the leaves, which occurs due to the low water potential of air. The driving force for translocation is the different hydrostatic pressure in areas of phloem near sources and sinks, which is caused by the active transport mechanism that pumps sugars.

- Fluid in phloem is under positive pressure, while fluid in xylem is under negative pressure. Stick a pin into phloem tissue and fluid squirts out. Stick a pin in xylem tissue and air is sucked in.

The evidence for translocation in phloem

The evidence that sucrose is transported in phloem comes from **radioactive tracers** and ringing experiments. If a plant is grown in an atmosphere with radioactively-labelled carbon dioxide (using the isotope carbon-14), the fate of the radioactive substance can be traced through the plant. As the plant photosynthesises the carbon-14 is initially found in glucose in the leaf, then it is found in sucrose in the phloem and finally ends up as starch in the sinks. The rate of movement of the radioactively-labelled carbon-14 is much faster than could be explained by other mechanisms, such as diffusion. This provides clear evidence for mass flow (translocation in phloem) as the mechanism for transporting the products of photosynthesis.

In trees, the phloem tissue is the innermost layer of the bark, while the active xylem is the outermost layer of the inner wood. If a ring of bark is removed right round the circumference of the tree, the phloem pathway is completely cut off. When this happens, sucrose accumulates above the ring, sometimes causing a bulge, suggesting the phloem transport sugars down the plant.

> **Notes**
> Revise water potential from Topic 2, section 3.2.3 to help you with this section.

31

3.4 Genetic information, variation and relationships between organisms

3.4.1 DNA, genes and chromosomes

In **eukaryotic cells** the DNA is linear and attached to organising proteins called **histones**, like cotton round a bobbin, as seen in Fig 26. In **prokaryotic cells** (bacteria) the DNA is organised in a completely different way; it is circular (in a loop) and not attached to histones.

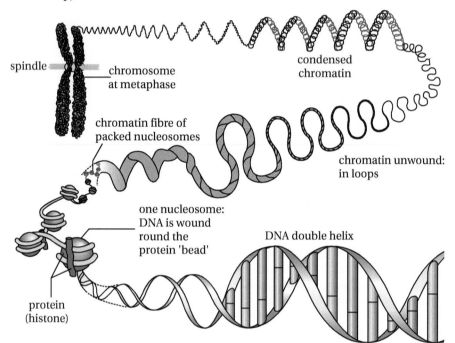

spindle
chromosome at metaphase
condensed chromatin

chromatin fibre of packed nucleosomes

chromatin unwound: in loops

one nucleosome: DNA is wound round the protein 'bead'

DNA double helix

protein (histone)

Fig 26
Each chromosome is one long supercoiled DNA molecule

What are genes?

The definition of a gene is central to this topic. **A gene is a base sequence of DNA (deoxyribonucleic acid) that codes for the amino acid sequence of a particular polypeptide or a functional RNA.** At A-level, if you think 'one gene makes one protein' you won't go far wrong.

The position of a particular gene on a chromosome is known as its **locus**. The plural of locus is **loci**.

The genetic code

The central dogma (idea) of biology is:

$$DNA \rightarrow RNA \rightarrow protein$$

DNA is used to make RNA which, in turn, is used to make proteins. The big question is: How?

The genetic code is the sequence of bases in DNA. This sequence codes for the order of amino acids in a polypeptide or protein. A *gene* is a length of DNA

> **Notes**
>
> Learn the definition of a gene. You may have been taught that genes control features such as eye colour and hair colour but in reality genes make proteins (including lots of different enzymes). It is those proteins that make the hair and eye colour, and all the other observable features.

that contains all the codons needed to synthesise a particular polypeptide or protein. So how is the genetic code used to build proteins?

There are only four bases (C, A, T and G) but 20 different amino acids, so:

- One base cannot code for one amino acid.

- A two-base code would give $4 \times 4 = 16$ combinations, which is still not enough.

- A three-base code gives $4 \times 4 \times 4 = 64$ possible different combinations, which is more than enough.

Definition

*A group of three bases in DNA or RNA that codes for a particular amino acid is known as a **codon**.*

One codon codes for one amino acid. For example, the codon AAA codes for the amino acid phenylalanine. As there are 64 codons, some amino acids are coded for by more than one. Some codons act as a 'full stop' to stop the amino acid chain growing further.

The genetic code is described as:

- **Universal** – in all organisms the same codons code for the same amino acids.

- **Non–overlapping** – successive codons are read in order, and each **nucleotide** is part of only one **triplet** codon. For example, the sequence ACTGGA is just two codons, ACT and GGA, not four, as in ACT, CTG, TGG and GGA, because there is no overlap.

- **Degenerate code** – there are more codons than necessary to code for the 20 amino acids. Consequently, some amino acids are coded by several different codons (see Table 4).

Ala	GCU, GCC, GCA, GCG	Leu	UUA, UUG, CUU, CUC, CUA, CUG
Arg	CGU, CGC, CGA, CGG, AGA, AGG	Lys	AAA, AAG
Asn	AAU, AAC	Met	AUG
Asp	GAU, GAC	Phe	UUU, UUC
Cys	UGU, UGC	Pro	CCU, CCC, CCA, CCG
Gln	CAA, CAG	Ser	UCU, UCC, UCA, UCG, AGU, AGC
Glu	GAA, GAG	Thr	ACU, ACC, ACA, ACG
Gly	GGU, GGC, GGA, GGG	Trp	UGG
His	CAU, CAC	Tyr	UAU, UAC
Ile	AUU, AUC, AUA	Val	GUU, GUC, GUA, GUG
START	AUG	STOP	UAG, UGA, UAA

Table 4
The mRNA codons that specify particular amino acids

Notes

You will never have to learn any examples of particular triplets and their amino acids – the exam questions will always provide them for you.

You will *not* be expected to remember these codons for the exam.

NB: All polypeptide chains are assembled starting with a methionine, which is why the start codon and methionine are the same.

Essential Notes

The hormone insulin, for example, consists of 51 amino acids and so the insulin gene has at least 51 codons, or $51 \times 3 = 153$ bases.

There are in fact four reasons why the insulin gene is longer than 153 bases:

1 A start codon

2 A stop codon

3 One or more introns

4 Insulin is in fact made as a longer polypeptide, called pro-insulin, and is activated in the Golgi body when the extra amino acids are removed.

Fig 27
Even in a gene, there are non-coding lengths of DNA called introns. Only the exons are encoded into the mRNA molecule, and therefore expressed.

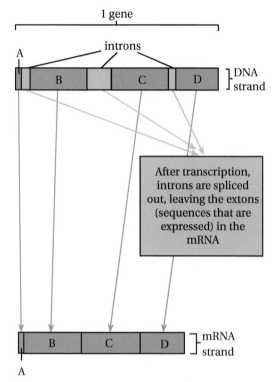

As Fig 27 shows, genes occur at particular places along a DNA molecule. There is a lot of non-coding DNA in between the genes, which may or may not have an important function – it's just another aspect of the human **genome** that we don't yet fully understand. Often the non-coding DNA consists of the same base sequence occurring again and again, known as **multiple repeats**, and the differences in this non-coding DNA form the basis of DNA profiling in forensics.

The genes themselves also contain some non-coding DNA. These base sequences do not contribute to the polypeptide, and are called **introns**. When a gene is transcribed the intron must be removed, leaving only the sequences to be **expressed** – the **exons**. The removal of introns is known as **splicing**.

3.4.2 DNA and protein synthesis

The **genome** is the entire DNA sequence of an organism; that is, all of the genes and, as we shall see in section 3.8.4, all of the non-coding DNA in between. The **proteome** is the full range of proteins that a cell is able to produce.

The base sequence of a gene codes for the amino acid sequence in a protein. You may remember that this is known as the **primary structure** of the protein.

When amino acids are joined together in a particular order, a whole range of forces will combine to fold, twist and bend the polypeptide chain into the most stable shape. This is the **tertiary structure** of the protein. In the case of an enzyme, the tertiary structure will include the active site, which is complementary to the substrate.

How is the genetic code in DNA used to build a protein? There are two stages:

1 **Transcription**

2 **Translation.**

> **Definition**
>
> *Transcription is the first stage in protein synthesis. The base sequence on a particular gene is copied onto molecules of mRNA (messenger RNA). This takes place in the nucleus.*

The mRNA molecules are effectively mobile copies of genes. They carry the code out of the nucleus to the site of translation, on the **ribosomes** in the cytoplasm.

> **Definition**
>
> *Translation is the second stage in protein synthesis. The base sequence on the mRNA molecule is used to assemble a protein. This takes place on ribosomes.*

Structure of RNA

RNA stands for ribonucleic acid. There are several types of RNA, two of which have a central role in protein synthesis:

- **Messenger RNA (mRNA)** is a single, long strand of nucleotides that is a copy of a gene (Fig 28).

- **Transfer RNA (tRNA)** is a small, cloverleaf-shaped molecule that brings particular amino acids to the ribosome during translation.

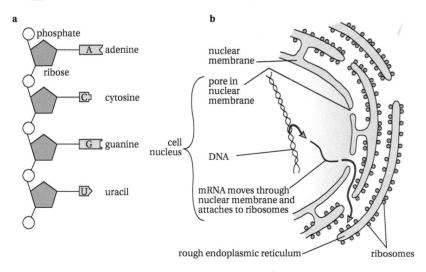

a phosphate
ribose
A adenine
C cytosine
G guanine
U uracil

b nuclear membrane
pore in nuclear membrane
cell nucleus
DNA
mRNA moves through nuclear membrane and attaches to ribosomes
rough endoplasmic reticulum
ribosomes

Fig 28
a The structure of a short section of mRNA (messenger RNA)
b Protein synthesis in the cell – transcription happens in the nucleus, while translation happens on the ribosomes

The essential differences between DNA, mRNA and tRNA are summarised in Table 5.

Table 5
A comparison of DNA, mRNA and tRNA. Note that these are RNA codons that have been transcribed from DNA

	DNA	mRNA	tRNA
Sugar	Deoxyribose	Ribose	Ribose
Bases	C, G, A and T	C, G, A and U	C, G, A and U
Strands	Double	Single	Single
Shape of molecule	Very long, double helix	Single unfolded strand	Strand folded back on itself, forming a 'cloverleaf'
Life span	Long term	Short term	Short term
Site of action	Nucleus	Nucleus and cytoplasm	Cytoplasm

The process of transcription

Most cells in the human body contain two complete sets of genes. However, only a few genes are used – or *expressed* – in any particular cell. For example, every cell in the human body contains two copies of the gene that codes for insulin, but only certain cells in the pancreas use the gene to make insulin.

The steps in transcription

There are three steps in the process of transcription (Fig 29):

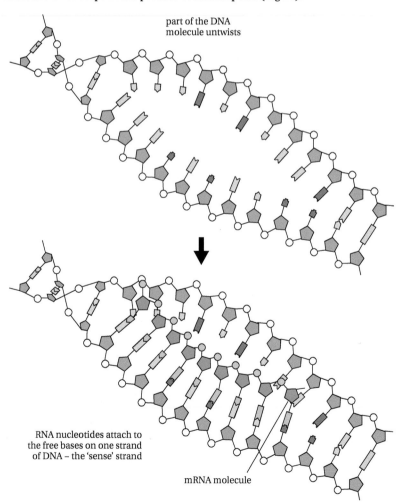

part of the DNA molecule untwists

RNA nucleotides attach to the free bases on one strand of DNA – the 'sense' strand

mRNA molecule

Fig 29
The process of transcription

- **Step 1** – the two strands of DNA unwind along the length of the gene. This is catalysed by enzymes.

- **Step 2** – the enzyme **RNA polymerase** moves along one side of the DNA molecule – the *sense strand* that contains the genetic code. The enzyme catalyses the assembly of an mRNA molecule by the addition of matching nucleotides. When RNA is synthesised, the base *thymine* is replaced by *uracil*, so the base pairing in RNA is always A with U and C with G.

- **Step 3** – the mRNA molecule peels off the gene and passes out of the nucleus.

Translation

Transfer RNA is the molecule that transfers amino acids to ribosomes during translation. It links the genetic code to the protein. At one end of the molecule is the **anticodon** which binds to the codon on the mRNA. At the other end is the amino acid specified by the codon (Fig 30).

A ribosome can be thought of as a giant enzyme that holds together all the components needed for translation (Fig 31):

- **Step 1** – the mRNA attaches itself to a ribosome.

- **Step 2** – the first codon is translated. The first codon is usually AUG, which codes for the amino acid methionine, so a tRNA molecule with the anticodon UAC will attach, carrying a methionine molecule at the other end.

- **Step 3** – the second codon is translated in the same way. The second amino acid is held alongside the first, and a peptide bond is formed by condensation between them. The polypeptide chain has started. ATP is split to provide the energy to form the peptide bond.

- **Step 4** – the process is repeated – the mRNA moves along the ribosome until the polypeptide has been built. If a stop codon is encountered, translation ceases and the polypeptide is finished.

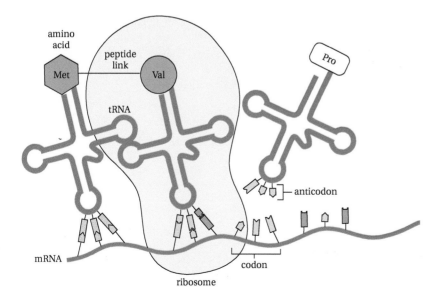

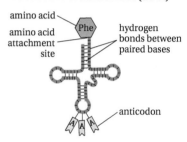

Fig 30
The structure of transfer RNA (tRNA)

Fig 31
The overall process of translation. The ribosome is not to scale.

Once the protein/polypeptide has been assembled, it folds and bends into its tertiary structure and accumulates on the inside of the rough endoplasmic reticulum. Here it is packaged into vesicles (spheres of membrane) and may pass to the Golgi apparatus where it is modified and/or activated. Some proteins are used inside the cells, and some are for export in which case they leave the cell by exocytosis.

3.4.3 Genetic diversity can arise as a result of mutation or during meiosis

Causes of variation

Ultimately, **mutation** is the source of all variation. A gene mutation is a change in the base sequence of the DNA. When a mutated gene is used in **protein synthesis**, there will probably be a change in the amino acid sequence. The amino acid chain will fold and bend into a differently shaped protein. The change in protein structure is usually harmful or neutral, but occasionally beneficial. Such beneficial mutations give an individual a selective advantage – this is the driving force behind evolution.

Gene mutation

> **Essential Notes**
>
> This section deals only with *gene* mutations. There are also chromosome mutations that involve fragments of chromosomes – whole blocks of genes – being lost or duplicated. Think of gene mutations as putting the wrong word into a book, while a chromosome mutation is the loss of a whole chapter.

A gene mutation occurs when there is a change in the sequence of bases, such as when a gene is copied incorrectly. This can result in one or more incorrect amino acids being incorporated into the protein. For example, if a codon that read AAA was copied incorrectly so that it read AAC, then asparagine would replace lysine (look back at Table 4 in section 3.4.1).

Gene mutation can happen in three different ways:

- substitution (or point mutation)
- addition
- deletion.

Substitution is where the wrong base is inserted.

For example, consider the base sequence:

AAT CGG CCC GTA

This will be transcribed into mRNA as:

UUA GCC GGG CAU

Notes

Many exam questions ask you to explain how a tiny change like substitution can be lethal to an organism. Remember that the essential points are:
wrong base → different codon → wrong amino acid in protein → overall shape of protein altered so that it cannot function.

and then translated into the amino acid sequence:

> leucine-alanine-glycine-histidine

If one base is substituted, so that the DNA sequence now reads:

> AAT C<u>A</u>G CCC GTA

the second codon will be transcribed as GUC which translates into the amino acid valine. So valine will replace alanine in the amino acid chain. This change to the primary structure of the protein might or might not affect the way the polypeptide chain folds and bends to produce the tertiary structure. If the new amino acid significantly changes the tertiary and/or quaternary structure (that is, the overall shape) the protein might not be able to function properly.

Addition is when an extra base is added into the sequence. All the bases that follow in the sequence are moved along. This is known as a **frame shift**. Addition could cause the sequence:

> ATT CGG CCC GTA

to become:

> AT<u>C</u> TCG GCC CGT

This will cause most of the amino acids coded for by codons at or after the addition to change, which, in turn, will produce a protein with a completely different primary structure.

A **deletion** involves the loss of a base, causing a frame shift in the other direction as all the bases move along to replace the one that was lost. This will also change most of the codons at or after the deletion. Overall, additions and deletions are more disruptive than substitutions.

Gene mutations can have one of three consequences:

- **They might be lethal**. The new amino acid causes the protein to be significantly different to the original, so that it does not perform its function in the organism (see Table 6). For instance, it might mean that the active site of an enzyme is the wrong shape to combine with the substrate. This might result in a *metabolic block*, in which the enzyme cannot play its part in a sequence of reactions, so that essential products are in short supply while intermediate compounds build up. Mutations that cause frame shifts are more likely to be lethal than substitutions because they change more codons, and thus more amino acids, such as the active site of an enzyme. A protein is more likely to function with one amino acid change than with a whole new sequence.

- **They might have no effect**. The protein might still function despite the new amino acid because the change does not alter the tertiary structure or the shape of the part of the protein which interacts with other chemicals, such as the active site of an enzyme. Also, because some amino acids are coded for by several different codons, a mutation might not result in a change in the amino acid.

- **They might be beneficial**. The new amino acid might alter the protein in such a way that it works in a different way - one that helps the organism.

What causes mutations?

Mutations normally occur by chance, just random mistakes in the copying of DNA, although the rate of mutation can be greatly increased by **mutagens.** These include:

- ultraviolet light

- X-rays

- α, β and γ radiation

- chemicals such as mustard gas and cigarette smoke.

Table 6 lists some examples of lethal gene mutations.

Table 6

Examples of lethal gene mutations

Disease	Function of healthy allele	Consequence of mutant allele
Cystic fibrosis	CFTR gene codes for a protein that transports ions across lung membranes, leading to normal watery mucus	No ion transport, so mucus becomes thick and sticky; lungs are easily infected
Haemophilia	Codes for Factor VIII, an essential protein in the chain reaction leading to blood clotting	Leads to a fault in the blood-clotting mechanism; even minor cuts lead to major blood loss
Phenylketonuria (PKU)	Codes for an enzyme that converts the amino acid phenylalanine into tyrosine	An example of a lethal metabolic block – phenylalanine and other related substances build up, interfering with brain development in the baby

Essential Notes

It's a bit like a pack of playing cards. Mutation creates new cards, and the three other processes shuffle the pack.

Mutation creates new alleles, but there are three more processes that also increase variation in organisms by creating *new combinations of alleles*:

1 Crossover in meiosis.

2 Independent assortment in meiosis.

3 **Random fertilisation** of **gametes** – in animals, all sperm and ova are genetically unique, and which sperm happens to fertilise the egg is totally random.

Meiosis

Notes

Many candidates lose marks by stating that all organisms have 23 pairs of chromosomes. Never mention the number 23 unless the question is specifically about humans.

First, four vital definitions:

- **Diploid** = A cell/organism which contains two sets of chromosomes. It is written as $2n$. For example, in humans $2n = 46$. Different species have different numbers of chromosomes.

- **Haploid** = A cell/organism which contains a single set of chromosomes. Shown as n, e.g. $n = 23$.

- **Mitosis** = Cell division in which cells are copied. One diploid cell gives rise to two identical diploid cells (or, more rarely, one haploid cell gives rise to two haploid cells)
- **Meiosis** = Cell division that shuffles the genes on the chromosomes so that all cells produced are genetically different. One diploid cell gives rise to *four* haploid cells.

You can see from the last definition that there are two key features to meiosis:

- It creates genetic variation.
- It halves the number of chromosomes in the cell.

It is therefore completely different from mitosis, which does neither. Let's look at it in more detail, using humans as an example

Every diploid human cell has 23 pairs of chromosomes. These pairs are **homologous**, which is another way of saying they have the same genes in the same positions but the alleles of those genes may differ. This is shown in Fig 32.

Meiosis is illustrated in Fig 33.

Meiosis produces variation in two ways:

1. In **crossover**, blocks of genes are swapped between homologous chromosomes (Fig 34). This produces variation because the crossover points – called **chiasmata** – occur at random. The result is that, although each chromosome still has a full set of genes, it may well have *new and different combinations of alleles*. This prevents the same set of alleles being passed down unchanged from generation to generation.

2. **Independent assortment** – the haploid cells contain *one* member from each homologous chromosome pair, but the choice of which member is purely random. In a cell with 23 pairs of chromosomes, there are 2^{23} different combinations of chromosomes, which is over 8 million.

Chromosome number

Meiosis must happen normally for the number of chromosomes to be maintained (after fertilisation). In humans, for example, cells with 46 chromosomes undergo meiosis to produce gametes with 23 chromosomes, so the normal diploid number of 46 is restored at fertilisation. However, a relatively common fault in meiosis is **non-disjunction**, in which one or more pairs of chromosomes fails to separate (in anaphase 1), so that one gamete gets both chromosomes while the other gets neither. The most common cause of Down's syndrome is non-disjunction of chromosome 21 so that some ova (eggs) get two chromosomes at position 21. If this ovum is fertilised, the resulting embryo has three chromosome 21s. This can also happen due to the sperm having two chromosome 21s, but this seems to be rarer.

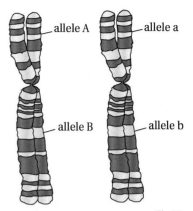

allele A   allele a

allele B   allele b

Fig 32
In diploid cells, chromosomes occur in pairs so that every cell has two alleles of each gene. Note that the bands are not all alleles. The bands just appear when the chromosomes are stained, the alleles are much smaller.

Notes

Don't confuse meiosis with mitosis. Remember: **Meiosis Makes Eggs In Ovaries, Sperm In Scrotum**. (It's not strictly true for all types of organism, but it does help to focus the mind.)

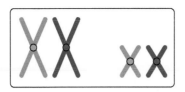

Early in the first meiotic division, homologous chromosomes pair up and lie alongside each other.

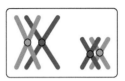

Crossover takes place. Chiasmata form and blocks of genes are swapped between material and paternal chromosomes.

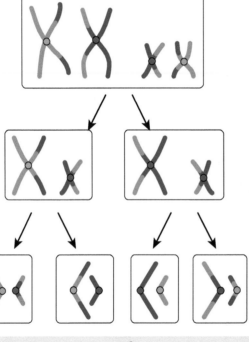

Result of crossover: each chromosome now has new allele combinations

FIRST MEIOTIC DIVISION
Independent assortment has taken place: one from each pair has gone into the daughter cell. The combination shown is just 1 of the 2 possible.

Fig 33
An overview of meiosis showing two pairs of homologous chromosomes

SECOND MEIOTIC DIVISION
The chromatids have been pulled apart, as in mitosis. End result: 4 daughter cells, all haploid, all genetically unique.

a

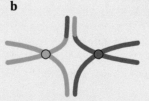

b

c

a
Homologous chromosomes lie alongside each other. They joint at points called chiasmata (singular = chiasma).

b
When the chromosomes separate blocks of genes have been swapped between maternal and paternal chromosomes. New combinations of alleles have been created.

c
The homologous chromosomes are pulled apart, and one goes to each daughter cell.

Fig 34
Crossover takes place during the first meiotic division.

3.4.4 Genetic diversity and adaptation

Random mutation can result in new alleles of a gene. The mutation may be beneficial, and confer a *selective advantage* on the individual. Individuals that have a selective advantage are more likely to survive and reproduce, passing their alleles or allele combinations on to the next generation.

A classic example of a beneficial mutation is seen in the peppered moth. The speckled variety of this moth was common in the UK before the time of the Industrial Revolution. Its speckled colouration gave it camouflage on light-coloured, lichen-covered rocks and tree bark. However, the industrial processes of the Industrial Revolution covered many surfaces with a layer of soot – the speckled moths stood out and were seen more easily by predators. A chance mutation in a gene (not *caused* by the soot) created an allele that caused a change in colouration, producing a black (melanic) variety of moth. The mutants were better camouflaged on sooty surfaces and so had a selective advantage. With every generation, the frequency of the melanic allele increased, and the melanic form became more common in sooty areas than the speckled form.

Natural selection

Natural selection is one of the most powerful and important ideas in science. The essential principles are:

- There is always variation in a population because different individuals possess different alleles.

- Some alleles or allele combinations will give the organism a selective advantage.

- Those individuals will have a better chance of passing on their alleles to the next generation. They will have greater reproductive success.

- In this way, the frequency of some alleles will increase over many generations, and some will decrease.

A good example of natural selection in action is that of **antibiotic resistance** in bacteria. Antibiotics are a large group of naturally occurring and synthesised drugs that combat bacterial infection. Antibiotics work by interfering with prokaryote metabolism but leave the eukaryotic cells of the host working normally.

As soon as there was wide-scale use of antibiotics, bacteria began developing resistance to them. Penicillin use began in 1942, and by 1947 there were reports of resistant strains of bacteria that did not respond to treatment. What the media call '**superbugs**' are strains of bacteria that are resistant to virtually all of the antibiotics at our disposal. They represent a growing threat to our health.

How does antibiotic resistance arise?

Initially, the resistance probably arose as a result of a mutation. A single gene in a bacterium mutated into a new allele, which produced a protein that in some way made the bacterium resistant to the antibiotic. The resistance alleles were transmitted from mother cell to daughter cells in mitosis. Bacteria can also pass resistance alleles from one to another by swapping **plasmids**, even with a bacterium of a different species. This helps to spread antibiotic resistance between bacterial populations.

Notes

Populations contain individuals with many different mutations that have accumulated over time. A change in the environment – such as a new antibiotic – will make a particular mutation relevant. Students often lose marks by stating that organisms mutate in *response* to the change.

Notes

A common mistake is to imply that the bacteria 'decide' to become resistant. The resistance alleles are already present in some fortunate individuals, or a very timely mutation produces a resistance allele by chance.

The resistant bacteria multiply, while the susceptible bacteria are killed. In this way, the frequency of the resistance allele increases over time. It is important to note that the antibiotic *did not cause* the mutation, which must have already existed in the population; or it occurred in the right place at the right time, to give the individual bacterium a selective advantage.

Directional and stabilising selection

The increase in frequency of the antibiotic resistance allele in bacteria is an example of **directional selection**. Directional selection occurs when the environment changes and the existing most common type may no longer have a selective advantage.

Another type of selection is **stabilising selection**, which illustrates the important idea that natural selection is not always a force for change.

In stabilising selection, the extremes of **phenotype** are at a disadvantage compared with the mid-range. The result is a reduction in variation. The classic example of this is human birth weight. Very small babies are at a disadvantage for a variety of reasons, from a weakened immune system to problems with temperature control. Very large babies cause problems in childbirth. In this way, natural selection favours mid-weight babies. Stabilising selection is probably the commonest type of selection.

Investigating the effect of antimicrobial substances on microbial growth

When working with bacteria or other potentially dangerous **microorganisms**, care must be taken to make sure that none of the microbes being used can escape, and that no microbes from the outside world can get in and contaminate our samples. The **aseptic technique** is a series of protocols (standardised procedures) that ensure no contamination in either direction.

Nutrient agar is a gel or a broth that is commonly used for growing microbes. Agar itself is a polysaccharide, obtained from seaweed, which has relatively little nutritional value. In order to grow microbes, nutrients are added to the agar. When bacteria are incubated at a suitable temperature, one bacterium can grow into a visible colony of bacteria within a few hours.

A bacterial lawn is prepared by smearing bacteria over the whole surface of agar in a petri dish. A sample of the antimicrobial compounds – such as antibiotics or disinfectants – is placed on the agar and the plate is incubated, commonly at 30°C for 24 hours. The effectiveness of the substance can be gauged from the size of the clear zone, because this is the area where no bacteria grew. We cannot say that they were killed, but they certainly have not reproduced.

Fig 35
Five paper discs soaked in a different antibiotic have been placed on an ager plate, flooded with a bacterial culture and incubated to grow a 'bacterial lawn'. The clear zone is where bacterial growth has been inhibited. In this case antibiotic 5 would seem to be the most effective against this particular bacterial species.

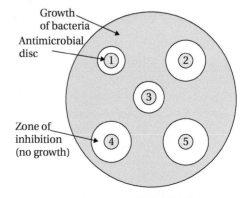

3.4.5 Species and taxonomy

There are, at present, over two million different species that have been discovered and therefore given a **scientific name**. Many more are yet to be classified.

The science of classification is known as **taxonomy**, and it aims to produce a catalogue of all living things on Earth, and as complete a picture of evolution as possible. This is not easy. This is one area of science where there is very little agreement. Systems and ideas are constantly changing as new evidence comes to light.

To set the scene:

- The Earth is very old – 4,600,000,000 (4.6 billion) years old is our current best estimate.
- Life probably evolved about 3.5 billion years ago.
- The extinct species greatly outnumber the living ones.
- Most species, especially the soft-bodied ones, did not leave fossils.
- Organisms did not evolve according to neat patterns and systems for the convenience of scientists.
- New evidence is coming to light all the time. Modern techniques including genome sequencing and protein analysis (see section 3.4.7) throw new light on evolutionary relationships, so that our ideas about what evolved from what, and what is related to what, are constantly changing.

What is a species?

A useful working definition of a species is:

A group of individuals that have observable similarities and the ability to interbreed and produce fertile offspring.

This definition works well enough for most situations, including A-level examinations. Lions and tigers can mate to produce ligers or tigons, while horses and donkeys can produce mules, but in all cases the hybrid offspring are infertile.

However, there are problems with this definition. Domestic dogs, wolves and coyotes can all interbreed to produce perfectly fertile offspring, and there are many other examples. The problem lies partly in the process of speciation, which can take time, and partly from our desire to give things precise definitions.

A better definition of a species is therefore:

A group of organisms that have similar physical, behavioural and biochemical features, that can interbreed to produce fertile offspring, and that do not normally interbreed with any other group of organisms.

Notes

The idea of speciation (the production of a new species) will be introduced in A-level, Topic 7.

Courtship behaviour is a necessary precursor to successful mating

Courtship behaviour enables animals to achieve several things:

- To recognise and seek out a member of the same species
- To approach a potential mate safely and without aggression
- To choose a strong and healthy mate
- To form a pair bond and synchronise breeding behaviour.

1. Species recognition

   This is important when closely related species are found together. Think of butterflies, birds, insects and frogs in a tropical rainforest. Strategies that ensure the same species mate include courtship displays and dances, mating calls and pheromones (chemical signals). Firefly species even have their own particular sequence of flashes.

2. Avoiding aggression

   When not mating, most animals have an individual space that reduces the risk of aggression and also reduces the spread of disease. Courtship enables this space to be invaded without triggering aggression.

3. Choosing a strong and healthy mate

   Breeding is a major investment of time and energy. Before mating, animals can improve their chances of reproductive success by selecting a mate that is fit and healthy. Some female birds, such as terns, test out the suitability of a potential mate by inviting him to feed her. If he can deliver plenty of fish, she will mate with him.

4. Forming a pair bond

   There are many species that form pair bonds, because it is one strategy that increases the chances of survival of the offspring. All animals invest a lot of energy in reproduction. At one end of the scale is the salmon, which lays a huge number of eggs and promptly dies. At the other end of the scale are animals such as humans that have very few offspring but invest a lot of energy in parental care.

Phylogenetic classification

All species are given a scientific name, which usually comes from Latin or Greek. This name is used across all language barriers, and avoids confusion when referring to a particular species.

Scientific names are **binomial** – they have two parts. The first part, the **generic name**, is the name of the **genus** and has a capital letter. The **specific name** follows, and does not have a capital letter. For example, *Canis familiaris* is the domestic dog, while *Gorilla gorilla* is (unsurprisingly) the gorilla. Scientific names should be given in italics or underlined.

This is described as a **phylogenetic** system of classification – it is one based on evolutionary history. It's a bit like a family tree that goes back millions of years. To construct a phylogenetic tree, scientists use anatomical/physical features, fossil records and, increasingly, biochemical analysis of DNA and proteins (see below).

The taxonomy uses a layered structure or **hierarchy**, one version of which is shown in Table 7. Its key features are:

- It consists of a series of groups within groups, from the most general (domain) to the most specific (species).

- There is no overlap between the groups. For instance, there is no organism that is part amphibian and part reptile – it is either in one group or the other.

- The groups are based on shared features. The more specific the group, the more shared features there are.

Notes

It may help to invent a mnemonic to remember the sequence of domain, kingdom, phylum etc. Make up a phrase according to DKPCOFGS, such as Don't Keep Putting Cabbages On Fat Greasy Slugs, or something more memorable/ silly/ personal to you.

Taxon	Humans as an example	Explanation
Domain	Eukaryota	Our cells have a nucleus and other membrane-bound organelles
Kingdom	Animalia	We are animals: generally, multicellular organisms that move in search of food
Phylum	Chordates	We possess a backbone
Class	Mammals	We have warm blood, fur and feed our young on milk
Order	Primates	We have large brains, grasping hands, fingernails, binocular colour vision
Family	Hominids	Man-like creatures, only one species not extinct
Genus	Homo	Literally 'man'
Species	sapiens	Literally 'thinking'

Table 7
Taxonomic hierarchy. Many groups of organism do not fall neatly into these eight categories, hence the need for additional categories such as suborder and infraclass.

The overall organisation – nobody can agree!

Classification is a good example of how scientists work. Ideas and models are constantly being revised in the light of new evidence. For many years scientists have put organisms into two groups on the basis of their cellular organisation – the prokaryotes and the eukaryotes. Then some scientists argued that the prokaryotes should be split into two – the Eubacteria and Archaebacteria. At the moment there is some strong support for the idea that above the level of kingdom there are three **domains**, **Bacteria**, **Archaea** and **Eukarya /Eukaryota** (both terms are acceptable).

Some scientists have accepted a five-kingdom system of classification. All organisms can be placed into one of these five kingdoms. Four contain the eukaryotic organisms while a fifth contains the prokaryotes – the bacteria. Many other scientists feel that the prokaryotes should be split into two or more kingdoms. The four eukaryote kingdoms are Animals, Plants, Fungi and Protoctista.

3.4.6 Biodiversity within a community

The term **diversity** describes the extent to which different species form the community of an ecosystem. An ecosystem with a greater number of different species is more diverse than one that contains only a limited number of species.

Ecosystems can show a great range in diversity. Environments such as a coral reef or a rainforest show a high species diversity because conditions are generally favourable and stable. In these situations biotic factors – those due to other organisms – dominate organisms' lives. In contrast, in harsh environments such as the arctic or desert regions, there is low species diversity and abiotic factors dominate, usually temperature and water availability.

Human activity can have an adverse effect on diversity. The following agricultural practices have all been shown to reduce diversity:

- Concentrating on a small number of crops and growing these as large areas of **monoculture**
- Removing hedgerows and field boundaries to make maximum use of land area
- Draining marshy areas and removing unprofitable pockets of woodland
- Using large quantities of chemical fertilisers to obtain maximum yield
- Using pesticides to deal with the increased damage from insects, plant diseases and weeds that are the result of growing large areas of the same crop on the same land for many successive years.

Species richness

There are two different aspects to species diversity: **species richness** and **species evenness**. Species richness refers to the number of species present, while species evenness refers to the distribution of the numbers of individuals between the species.

For example, there might be six different species in an ecosystem, and the number of individuals are 980, 12, 4, 9, 21 and 15. Another ecosystem might have the same six species but the number of individuals is 150, 120, 260, 500, 300 and 220. The species evenness is much greater in the second ecosystem, even though the richness is the same. A community dominated by a few species is seen by biologists as less diverse than one in which many species are well represented.

Index of diversity

An **index of diversity** puts a numerical value on the number of species present in an ecosystem. It takes into account the number of individuals in each species in the community, the species richness. However, diversity depends not only on richness, but also on evenness. Evenness compares the similarity of the population size of each of the species present.

You need to know how to calculate a diversity index (d), using the formula:

$$d = \frac{N(N-1)}{\Sigma\, n(n-1)}$$

where N = total number of organisms of all species
and n = total number of organisms of each species
Σ = sum of all

The value we get represents the probability that, if we randomly choose two individuals, they will belong to distinct species. Thus the minimum value possible, 1, represents no diversity, increasing values represent increasing diversity, with maximum diversity getting 5.

As an example, Table 8 shows the number of different birds in a particular habitat.

Substituting the data into the above formula

$$d = \frac{24\,(23)}{176} = 3.136$$

So the diversity of this habitat is 3.136: a mid-range value.

Notes

You may read about the Simpson's diversity indices but it will always be Simpson's reciprocal index that you are asked about in AS/A2 exams.

Species	Number (n)	(n–1)	n(n–1)	Table 8
Chaffinch	2	1	2	
Great tit	6	5	30	
Sparrow	12	11	132	
Blue tit	4	3	12	
Total (Σ)	24	20	176	

3.4.7 Investigating diversity

Genetic diversity exists in two basic forms:

1 Variation between different species is interspecific variation.

2 Variation between members of a species is intraspecific variation.

DNA and protein analysis

Every living organism contains DNA, RNA and proteins. Closely related organisms generally have a high degree of similarity in the sequences of bases in DNA or mRNA or amino acid sequences, whereas the base sequences or amino acid sequences of distantly related organisms usually show fewer similarities. This is because mutations accumulate over time. Using DNA sequencing techniques it is possible to build 'relationship trees' that show the probable evolution of various organisms (Fig 36).

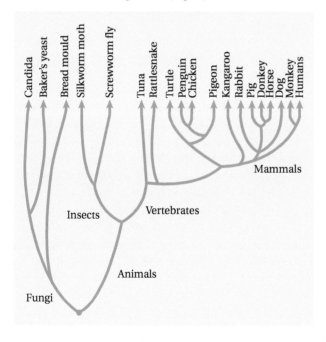

Fig 36
A phylogenetic tree based on the amino acid sequence data of cytochrome C. The relationship between the tuna, rattlesnake, turtle and three species of bird is surprising, and does not reflect the traditional view of things.

The differences between species are largely due to differences in their **DNA**. For example, DNA analysis shows that 98.6% of the DNA sequences found in humans and chimps are the same.

Quantitative investigations of variation

Normal distribution, mean and standard deviation

Measurable characteristics of a species, such as the height of individuals, usually varies. When such data is plotted on a graph a normal distribution is obtained (see Fig 37). Most individuals are in the middle, fewer at the extremes.

The **mean** is the arithmetic average. In the example shown in Fig 38, the mean height is 175 cm.

Standard deviation refers to the spread of the data around the mean, and is shown in the width of the curve. One standard deviation is the range on either side of the mean that contains 68% of the sample, and two standard deviations contain 95% of the sample. In Fig 38, you would write that the standard deviation in human male height is 175 cm ± 5 cm, which means that 68% of the male population falls in a 10 cm range from 170 to 180 cm.

Scientists have long been attempting to construct phylogenetic trees in an attempt to clarify the history of life on Earth. Early attempts were based on shared features, mainly anatomical. All scientists had to work on were living or preserved specimens, and fossils. Phylogenetic trees were constructed using shared features such as body plan, skeletal structure, and so on. In the last two decades, however, DNA sequencing technology has moved us into a new era.

Protein differences: what they can tell us about relationships between organisms

Proteins are made up of many amino acids, arranged in a specific sequence. The sequence of a particular protein is likely to be very similar in two closely related species, but may be different in two species that are separated by millions of years of evolution. So, comparing sequences in proteins that fulfil basic functions in the cell can tell us a lot about the path of evolution.

For example, scientists have looked at the protein **cytochrome c**, which is a protein that occurs on the surface of the inner membrane of the mitochondria. Because this protein is essential to the electron transfer reactions of respiration that take place there, it doesn't change very much over time. The only mutations that are possible are ones that do not affect its function.

Comparing cytochrome c sequences between species tells us whether they had a common ancestry, and how recently. For example, humans share exactly the same cytochrome c molecule with chimpanzees, but the protein in the rhesus monkey is different by one amino acid. A yeast has a cytochrome c that differs by 51 amino acids. Looking at the number of amino acid differences that exist between different species in different proteins can be used to construct very complex phylogenetic trees.

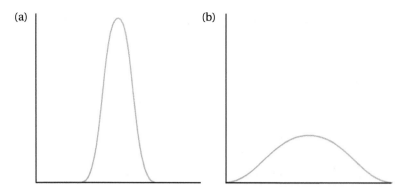

Fig 37
Different normal distribution curves.
   (a) A narrow distribution curve.
   (b) A wide distribution curve.
The standard deviation in graph (a) is much greater than in graph (b).

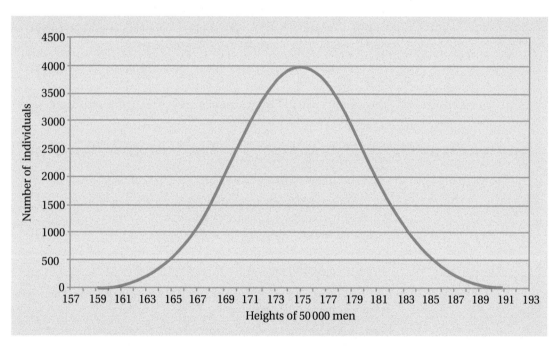

Fig 38 Height in human males is an example of continuous variation, shown graphically
as a bell-shaped curve known as a normal distribution. Environment also plays a part;
without adequate nutrition and health care, an individual will not reach their full height

Practical and mathematical skills

In both the AS and A level papers at least 15% of marks will be allocated to the assessment of skills related to practical work. A minimum of 10% of the marks will be allocated to assessing mathematical skills at level 2 and above. These practical and mathematical skills are likely to overlap to some extent, for example applying mathematical concepts to analysing given data and in plotting and interpretation of graphs.

The required practical activities assessed at AS are:

- Investigation into the effect of a named variable on the rate of an enzyme-controlled reaction
- Preparation of stained squashes of cells from plant root tips; setup and use of an optical microscope to identify the stages of mitosis in these stained squashes and calculation of a mitotic index
- Production of a dilution series of a solute to produce a calibration curve with which to identify the water potential of plant tissue
- Investigation into the effect of a named variable on the permeability of cell-surface membranes
- Dissection of animal or plant gas exchange system or mass transport system or of organ within such a system
- Use of aseptic techniques to investigate the effect of antimicrobial substances on microbial growth.

The additional required practical activities assessed only at A level are:

- Use of chromatography to investigate the pigments isolated from leaves of different plants, for example leaves from shade-tolerant and shade-intolerant plants or leaves of different colours
- Investigation into the effect of a named factor on the rate of dehydrogenase activity in extracts of chloroplasts
- Investigation into the effect of a named variable on the rate of respiration of cultures of single-celled organisms
- Investigation into the effect of an environmental variable on the movement of an animal using either a choice chamber or a maze
- Production of a dilution series of a glucose solution and use of colorimetric techniques to produce a calibration curve with which to identify the concentration of glucose in an unknown 'urine' sample
- Investigation into the effect of a named environmental factor on the distribution of a given species.

Questions will assess the ability to understand in detail how to ensure that the use of instruments, equipment and techniques leads to results that are as accurate as possible. The list of apparatus and techniques is given in the specification.

Exam questions may require problem solving and application of scientific knowledge in practical contexts, including novel contexts.

Exam questions may also ask for critical comments on a given experimental method, conclusions from given observations or require the presentation of data in appropriate ways such as in tables or graphs. It will also be necessary to express numerical results to an appropriate precision with reference to uncertainties and errors, for example in thermometer readings.

The mathematical skills assessed are given in the specification.

Practice exam-style questions

1   The bar graph shows some the main causes of death among UK males in 2001 and 2006.

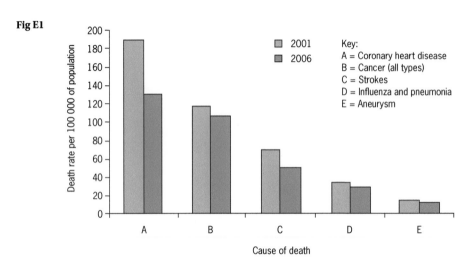

Fig E1

(a) Which category of disease, A–E, can be classed as a communicable disease?   1 mark

_____

(b) The population of the UK is 55 million. Calculate how many men died from coronary heart disease in 2006. Show your working.   2 marks

_____

_____

(c) List three risk factors associated with the development of coronary heart disease.   2 marks

_____

_____

_____

(d) Suggest two reasons for the reduction in the number of deaths, per 100 000 of population from heart disease from 2001 to 2006.   2 marks

_____

_____

_____

Total 7

2   The diagram shows the heart during a particular stage of the cardiac cycle.

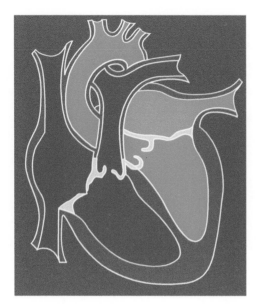

Fig E2

(a) Label:

   (i) the atrioventricular valves

   (ii) the aorta   2 marks

(b) Does this diagram show atrial systole or ventricular systole? Give one piece of evidence that supports your answer.   1 mark

_____

(c) Explain how a blood clot in a coronary artery may lead to a myocardial infarction.   2 marks

_____

_____

_____

Total 5

3 The diagram shows some of the changes as blood flows through different blood vessels.

Fig E3

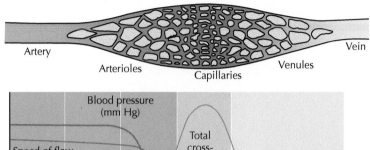

(a) Why are arteries and veins classed as organs but capillaries are not?

_____

_____

_____ 2 marks

(b) (i) Explain why blood pressure is high in the arteries.

_____ 1 mark

(ii) Explain why blood pressure drops as blood flows from the large arteries through the capillaries.

_____

_____ 2 marks

(c) Describe and explain the relationship between total cross-sectional area and speed of flow.

_____

_____

_____ 2 marks

(d) Explain how each of the following contributes to the efficient exchange of substances between blood and tissues:

  (i) The speed of flow.

  (ii) The structure of capillaries.

_____

_____ 2 marks

(e) Give two ways in which the flow of blood through the veins is maintained.

_____

_____ 2 marks

Total marks: 11

4   The table shows the results of a survey into the number of different small mammal species found in two different woodlands.

Species	Number of individuals	
	Woodland A	Woodland B
Woodmouse	15	14
Common shrew	3	8
Bank vole	17	9
Grey squirrel	9	12
Field vole	0	6
Common dormouse	0	2

The formula for diversity (d) is:

$$d = \frac{N(N-1)}{\Sigma n(n-1)}$$

where N = total number of organisms of all species

and n = total number of organisms of each species

Σ = sum of all

Use this formula to answer the questions.

(a) Explain what is meant by *diversity* in an ecosystem.

_____

_____ 2 marks

(b) Calculate a diversity index for Woodland A.

_____ 2 marks

(c) Suggest **two** human activities that could reduce the species diversity in Woodland A.

_____

_____ 2 marks

Total marks: 6

5   In an investigation into the properties of haemoglobin, researchers studied two species of Indian geese. The greylag goose lives at sea level all the year round, while the barheaded goose migrates up to Tibet, crossing the Himalayas at heights of up to 9000 metres. At that altitude, the partial pressure of oxygen is much lower than it is at sea level.

The graph shows the oxygen dissociation curve for the barheaded and greylag goose.

Fig E4

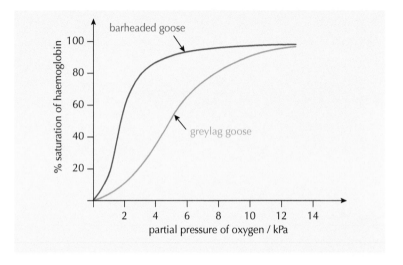

(a)   State and explain the differences between the oxygen dissociation curves for the barheaded goose and the greylag goose.

_____

_____ 2 marks

(b)   Explain what is meant by the Bohr effect.

_____

_____ 2 marks

(c)   Explain the importance of the Bohr effect on the delivery of oxygen to the tissues.

_____

_____ 2 marks

Tubifex, or sludge worms, contain haemoglobin. They live in poorly oxygenated water where they burrow into the mud, head first.

(d)   Explain why organisms like tubifex have haemoglobin.

_____ 1 mark

(e)   When oxygen concentrations are low, tubifex move out of their tubes and expose more of their bodies to the water. Explain how this helps them to gain oxygen.

_____ 2 marks

Total marks: 9

6 The diagram shows the adult of one species of tapeworm. These simple animals are parasites in the intestine, and have no organs of gas exchange, or a circulatory system.

Fig E5

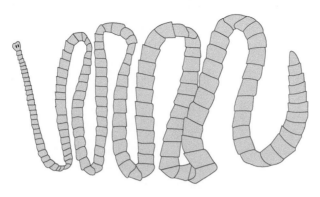

(a) Explain why the tapeworm doesn't need gas exchange organs.   2 marks

_____

_____

(b) Explain why the tapeworm doesn't need a circulatory system.   1 mark

_____

A spirometer is a device that measures the volume of air breathed in and out.

An athlete on an exercise bike was connected up to a spirometer and after a few minutes he began to exercise.

Pulmonary ventilation is calculated from the equation

pulmonary ventilation = breathing rate × tidal volume

	Pulmonary ventilation rate /cm^3 min^{-1}
At rest	7000
After 3 minutes of exercise	21 150

(c) Calculate the percentage increase in pulmonary ventilation rate after exercise.   1 mark

Answer = _____ %

his athlete had a measured tidal volume at rest of 500 cm^3. For an athlete with a tidal volume at rest of 450 cm^3, calculate the breathing rate they would need to maintain to achieve the same pulmonary ventilation rate at rest.

2 marks

Answer = _____ %

Total marks: 6

7   The **white-blooded icefish** are a family of fish that lack red blood cells. Only about 1% of their blood volume is composed of haemoglobin, compared with about 45% for most vertebrates. They have an almost transparent, flattened body and swim very slowly through the cold Antarctic waters.

The table below shows part of the classification of the icefish family.

Kingdom	Animalia
	Chordata
Class	Osteichthyes
	Perciformes
Family	Channichthyidae

(a)   Fill in the two missing levels.

1 mark

_____

(b)   What level of classification is above kingdom?

1 mark

_____

(c)   Which two levels of classification are below family?

1 mark

_____

(d)   Use the information given to explain how the icefish are able to survive without haemoglobin.

2 marks

_____

_____

Total marks: 5

8 Haemoglobin is a protein which is described as having a quaternary structure.

(a) Explain what is meant by quaternary structure. 1 mark

The graph shows the dissociation curve for adult and foetal haemoglobin. Before birth, a foetus must pick up oxygen from the placenta.

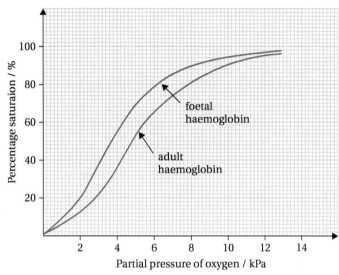

(b) The partial pressure at the placenta is 5 kPa. Use the graph to calculate the percentage transfer between the adult and foetal blood. 2 marks

Answer = _____ %

(c) Explain how haemoglobin is able to release oxygen to respiring tissues. 3 marks

Total marks: 6

9   Essay question

Variation between individuals of a particular species can be caused by genetic or environmental factors.

Write an essay on the genetic causes of variation within a species. Include a discussion of why this variation is important.   25 marks

Answers

Question	Answer	Marks
1 (a)	Influenza/pneumonia. (Flu is caused by a virus)	1
1 (b)	(130 deaths per hundred thousand $\times 10 \times 55$) = 71 500	2
1 (c)	Any three from; high blood pressure, obesity, smoking, high cholesterol, genetic predisposition.	2, one for two factors, two for three factors
1 (d)	Any two from; better education about risk avoidance, fewer smokers, more people exercising, earlier diagnosis and treatment.	2, one for each
		Total 7
2 (a) (i)	Correct label, one mark each	1
2 (a) (ii)		1
2 (b)	Ventricular systole. The atrioventricular valves are closed; The semilunar valves are open.	1
2 (c)	Any two from: Part of heart muscle starved of oxygen. Heart muscle dies (infarcts). Normal contraction not possible/conducting pathway blocked.	2
		Total 5
3 (a)	Capillaries are made from one type of specialised cell and are therefore classed as tissues. Arteries and veins are made more than one type of specialised cell/tissue and are therefore classed as organs.	2, one for each point
3 (b) (i)	They have just received blood from the left ventricles of the heart.	1
3 (b) (ii)	The elastic recoil (or elastic fibres) of the artery and arteriole walls absorbs the pressure/pulse wave.	2
3 (c)	Relationship: the greater the total cross-sectional area, the slower speed of flow. Explanation: there is more resistance to flow through capillaries/more friction between capillary wall and blood.	2, one for each point
3 (d) (i)	The slower flow gives more time for exchange/diffusion.	1
3 (d) (ii)	The permeable walls allow efficient exchange. OR Thin walls allow rapid diffusion.	1
3 (e)	Valves prevent backflow. (1) Large lumen minimises friction between blood and vessel wall. (1)	2
		Total 11
4 (a)	A measure of the number of different species (1) in relation to the number of individuals. (1)	2
4 (b)	$d = 44(43)/[15(14) + 3(2) + 17(16) + 9(8) + 0(-1) + 0(-1)] = 3.38$	2

Question	Answer	Marks
4 (c)	Any two from: Removal of hedgerows; Monoculture; Pesticide spraying; Human activity/trampling; Deforestation	2, one for each point
		Total 6
5 (a)	Barheaded goose haemoglobin has a *higher affinity* for oxygen. (1) It can, therefore, bind to O_2 even at low partial pressures. (1)	2
5 (b)	Any two from: Carbon dioxide reduces the affinity of haemoglobin for oxygen; Carbon dioxide makes haemoglobin give up its oxygen; Carbon dioxide is acidic/acid de-stabilises Hb; Curve moves to the right.	2, one for each point
5 (c)	Oxygen will be released into the respiring tissue (1) that needs it most. (1)	2
5 (d)	To store oxygen in conditions of low oxygen tension.	1
5 (e)	Greater surface area (1) for absorption of oxygen. (1)	2
		Total 9
6 (a)	Any **two** from: Large surface area to volume ratio; Gas exchange over whole body surface; All cells close to exterior.	2
6 (b)	Either: No specialised organs of exchange (or words to that effect); Or: The needs of each cell are met by diffusion (or other cell transport processes)	1
6 (c)	(21 150 – 7000) / 7000 × 100 = 202%	1
6 (d)	breathing rate = pulmonary ventilation / tidal volume = 7000 / 450 = 15.6	2
		Total 6
7 (a)	Phylum, order	1
7 (b)	Domain	1
7 (c)	Genus, species	1
7 (d)	Any **two** from: Flattened shape means a large surface area to volume ratio; Short diffusion distance to most cells in the body in over all the body; Slow movement means low oxygen demand; Cold water means more oxygen dissolved than in warm water	2
		Total 5
8 (a)	It has more than one (i.e. four) polypeptide chains.	1
8 (b)	80 – 55 = 25% transfer	2
8 (c)	Any **three** from: Respiring cells make carbon dioxide; In red cells, the enzyme carbonic anhydrase stimulates the production of acid from carbon dioxide; Acid (or H^+ ions) lowers the affinity of haemoglobin; Haemoglobin dissociates / oxygen is free to diffuse.	3
		Total 6

Question	Answer	Marks
9	Essay mark scheme	
	There are **25 marks** for the essay and about 40 minutes to write it, and a good length essay is about three sides. So a rough guide is 5 minutes to plan and just over ten minutes a page.	
	The answer is marked using levels of response.	
		Level 5: 21–25 marks
	Answer is always clearly explained and there are no significant errors or irrelevant topics. All the topics are fully integrated with clear links made between topics. The content and terminology are detailed and comprehensive. For top marks, answers must show evidence of reading beyond the specific context of the specification requirements.	
		Level 4: 16–20 marks
	Answer is well organised with links that relate several topics to the main theme of the question. The explanations of each part are clear and generally correct in content and use of terminology. Most points are detailed. There may be one significant error or irrelevant topic.	
		Level 3: 11–15 marks
	The answer covers several suitable aspects but they are unrelated. Links are not made to the theme of the question. The explanations are clear and usually correct, and the content and terminology are at A level standard although the answer may lack detail. There may be some significant errors or more than one irrelevant topic.	
		Level 2: 6–10 marks
	The answer covers only one or a few aspects relevant to the question. The explanation of each part may be poor and lack detail. The answer shows limited use of appropriate terminology and there may be a number of significant errors or irrelevant topics.	
		Level 1: 1–5 marks
	The answer is unfocused – it includes some isolated biological facts but they are poorly explained and many may be factually incorrect. The content and terminology are generally below A level and may contain a large number of irrelevant topics.	
		Level 0: 0 marks
	Nothing of relevance	
	Relevant content includes:	
	• Mutation • Types of mutation (addition, substitution, deletion, frame shifts) • Consequences of mutation (effect on alleles) • Meiosis • Homologous chromosomes • Crossing-over • Independent segregation/assortment • Random fertilisation • Concept of the gene pool • Natural selection • Changes in allele frequency	

Glossary

Accuracy	A measure of how close the data is to the actual true value. Note the difference between accuracy and precision. If a man is 1.81m tall, a measurement of 1.743 m is precise but not accurate. The difference between accurate and precise is illustrated below:

   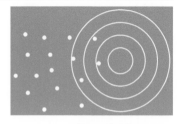

Precise-Accurate   Precise-Inaccurate   Imprecise-Accurate   Imprecise-Inaccurate

Addition	Type of gene mutation in which a base is added, causing a frame shift in one direction, so that many codons are changed. See also **deletion**, **substitution**, **mutation**.
Affinity	Degree of attraction. For example, haemoglobin has a high affinity for oxygen.
Allele	An alternative form of a gene. For example, a flower colour gene could have an allele for red flowers and one for white flowers.
Alveolar epithelium	A single layer of cells on the surface of alveoli.
Amino acid	Building block of a protein. There are 20 different amino acids in living things.
Amylase	Enzyme that breaks down (hydrolyses) starch to maltose.
Anomalous result	Measurement that falls outside the normal range of values. When many repeats are made, anomalous data can be identified more easily.
Antagonistic	Working against each other; for example, the actions of pairs of muscles, such as biceps and triceps in the upper arm.
Antibiotic	An anti-bacterial drug such as penicillin, tetracycline.
Antibiotic resistance	The ability of bacteria to resist the effects of an antibiotic.
Anticodon	Sequence of three bases found on a **transfer RNA** molecule, that codes for a specific amino acid. An anticodon binds to a complementary codon on messenger RNA (mRNA) during translation.
Archaea	In classification, one of the three domains, along with **Bacteria** and **Eukarya**. Once thought to be bacteria, Archaea are single-celled organisms without nuclei and with membranes that are different from all other organisms. They have a unique tough outer cell wall and protective enzymes that allow them to thrive in extreme conditions such as hot/acidic waters.

Aseptic technique	A set of procedures to control the opportunities for contamination of microbiology cultures by microorganisms from the environment, or contamination of the environment by the microorganisms being handled.
Atrioventricular node (AVN)	Part of the conducting pathway of the heart. The AVN picks up the signal from the sino-atrial node SAN, and delays it (allowing ventricles to fill) before passing it down into the bundle of His.
Bacteria	Simple, single-celled prokaryotic organism. Bacteria can be classed as one of the three domains. See also **Archaea** and **Eukarya**.
Base	In nucleic acids (DNA and RNA), one of four nitrogen-containing compounds, that fit together like jigsaw pieces. In DNA there are adenine, thymine, guanine and cytosine (C bonds to G, A to T). RNA has uracil (U) instead of thymine.
Bile	Substance secreted by the liver and released into the small intestine. Bile does not contain any enzymes, but it does contain bile salts to aid lipid digestion, and is alkaline to neutralise stomach acid.
Bile salts	Compounds in bile that have both hydrophilic and hydrophobic regions and help to emulsify fats.
Binomial	Having two names: the current classification system of species is binomial, for example, *Homo sapiens*.
Biodiversity	In conservation, a measure of the number of different species in a particular ecosystem. The influence of humans often reduces biodiversity.
Bohr effect	Name given to the fact that in the presence of carbon dioxide, the affinity of haemoglobin for oxygen is lower.
Bundle of His	Part of the conducting pathway of the heart: a bundle of specialised heart muscle fibres (*not* nerves) that transmit the impulse from the AVN to the Purkinje fibres.
Carbonic anhydrase	Enzyme that speeds up the reaction between carbon dioxide and water, forming carbonic acid, which then dissociates into H^+ and HCO_3^- ions. Particularly important in red blood cells, where the H^+ ions cause haemoglobin to release O_2.
Chiasmata	In meiosis, the points of crossover. In other words, sites where chromosomes break and join to others.
Chromosome	Condensed mass of DNA that appears just before cell division. Each chromosome is one super-coiled DNA molecule containing thousands of genes.
Chylomicron	Spheres consisting of a mixture of triglyceride, phospholipids, protein and cholesterol. They are formed in the endoplasmic reticulum of gut epithelial cells. The chylomicrons pass from the epithelial cells into the lacteals, and travel through the lymph system before joining the blood in the upper thorax.
Co-transport	Transport across a cell membrane in which the movement of one substance relies on the movement of another in the same direction. For example, glucose is co-transported with sodium.

Codon	A group of three bases in DNA or RNA that codes for a particular amino acid. Also called a **triplet**.
Cohesion tension	Mechanism by which water passes up the xylem of a plant, from roots to leaves. The cohesion of water allows continuous columns under great tension.
Constrict	To get smaller, as in vasoconstrict, when an arteriole gets narrower. NB: Only arterioles can do this, not veins, arteries or capillaries.
Counter-current system	When fluid flows in parallel tubes in opposite directions. Maximises efficiency of material exchange by maintaining a diffusion gradient along the whole length of the system. Maximises gas exchange in fish gills.
Crossover	In meiosis, the process that swaps blocks of genes between homologous chromosomes. Creates new combinations of alleles, so increasing variation.
Degenerate code	There are 64 different codons, but only 20 different amino acids, so some amino acids have several different codons.
Deletion	Type of gene mutation in which a base is lost (deleted). This causes a **frame shift**.
Diaphragm	The muscles between the thorax and the abdomen.
Diastole	Phase of the cardiac cycle in which the heart muscle is relaxed.
Dicotyledons	The largest group of flowering plants. Often shortened to dicot.
Diffusion	Molecular mixing, where particles in a gas or liquid move from an area of high concentration to an area of lower concentration until evenly spread.
Dilate	To get larger, as in vasodilate, when an arteriole expands its diameter.
Dipeptide	Molecule formed when two amino acids are joined by a peptide bond.
Diploid	A cell/organism which contains two sets of chromosomes. Shown as $2n$. For example, in humans, $2n = 46$. See also **haploid**.
Directional selection	A type of natural selection in which the selection pressure is shifted towards one end of a variation range by favouring more extreme phenotypes over others.
Disaccharide	Molecule formed when two monosaccharides join by a glycosidic bond. Common examples include maltose, lactose and sucrose.
Dissociation	Dis-association, in other words, coming apart. For example, when haemoglobin gives up its oxygen, or when an acid gives up an H^+ ion.
Diversity	A measure of the number of different species in a community.
DNA	Deoxyribonucleic acid.
Domain	Over-arching group in classification, above kingdom. See **Archaea**, **Bacteria** and **Eukarya**.
Endopeptidase	An enzyme that breaks peptide bonds in the middle of polypeptide chains.

Eukarya	The domain that contains the eukaryotes; animals, plants, fungi and protoctists. See also **Archaea**, **Bacteria**.
Eukaryotic cell	Cells with a true nucleus and DNA organised into chromosomes. Complex cell with organelles such as mitochondria, endoplasmic reticulum, and so on. Animals, plants and fungi are eukaryotic.
Exons	In a gene, the base sequences that are expressed, so used to make a polypeptide/protein. See also **introns**.
Exopeptidase	An enzyme that breaks peptide bonds at the ends of polypeptide chains.
Expressed	A gene is expressed when it is active and being used to make a particular protein/polypeptide.
Fatty acid	An organic acid containing a long, polar hydrocarbon chain with a –COOH group at one end. Fatty acids vary in the number of carbons in their chain and the degree of saturation (the number of C=C bonds). The formula of a fatty acid can be written as RCOOH, where R represents the hydrocarbon chain.
Frame shift	In mutation, a situation where a base is added or lost, causing all other bases to move along one place in a particular direction.
Gamete	A sex cell: sperm in males, eggs in females.
Gastric juice	The juice secreted by glands in the walls of the stomach, which destroys potentially harmful bacteria in food.
Gene	A length of DNA that codes for one protein or polypeptide.
Generic name	Name of the genus; first part of a scientific name. Always has capital: for example, *Homo* in *Homo sapiens*.
Genetic code	The base sequence of the DNA molecule. The code is copied onto molecules of mRNA and used as a template to make polypeptides/proteins.
Genome	The entire DNA sequences contained within the genetic material of an organism. The human genome consists of 3 billion base pairs; 30 000 genes on the 23 chromosomes, plus the non-coding DNA between the genes.
Genotype	The alleles that an organism has. Aa or AA, AaBb or Aabb and so on. Compare with phenotype.
Genus	Taxonomic grouping, more general than species but more specific than family. First part of the scientific name. For example, *Felis* is the genus in *Felis cattus* (cat).
Gill filaments	Supporting structures found in gills. In bony fish, four pairs of gill arches support many gill filaments, which in turn support the gill lamellae.
Gill lamellae	Small flat respiratory surfaces on gill filaments, the equivalent of alveoli in lungs.
Glycerol	A chemical that combines with three fatty acid molecules to form a lipid.

Haemoglobin	Protein found in the red blood cells of vertebrates, and in the body tissues of some invertebrates. Key function; storage and transport of oxygen; it binds to oxygen when abundant, and releases it when levels are low.
Haploid	A cell/organism that has a single set of chromosomes, for example, human eggs and sperm. Shown as *n*. For example, in human gametes, $n = 23$.
Hierarchy	In taxonomy, a layered system of groups within groups, with no overlap.
Histone	Class of protein that organises the DNA in the nucleus. DNA winds round a histone, like cotton round a bobbin.
Homeostasis	The maintenance of more or less stable conditions within the body. For example, temperature, blood glucose, pH, water potential.
Homologous chromosomes	A pair of chromosomes that have the same genes in the same places (loci) although not always the same alleles. Human females have 23 homologous pairs, while males have 22, because the X and Y chromosomes are not homologous.
Humidity	The amount of water vapour in the air. The lower the humidity, the greater the water potential gradient between a wet surface and the air, and the faster the rate of evaporation. Important in sweating (animals) and in transpiration (plants).
Hydrolase	General term for any enzyme that brings about a hydrolysis reaction. Most digestive enzymes are hydrolases.
Hydrolysis	Literally, 'splitting using water'. Digestion usually involves hydrolysis.
Hydrophilic	'Water-loving'; for example, the polar heads of a phospholipid.
Hydrophobic	'Water-hating'; for example, the non-polar tails of fatty acids.
Hydrostatic pressure	The physical pressure of fluid. Defined in biology as: Force per unit area exerted by a fluid (such as blood) against a vessel wall.
Hypothesis	An idea that it is possible to test with an experiment.
Independent assortment	A key feature of meiosis, which separates the homologous chromosomes so that any one of a pair of alleles can pass into a gamete with one from any other pair.
Index of diversity	A numerical value that reflects the number of different species in a community, in relation to the number of individuals. Used to compare the difference in diversity between two communities, or the change in a community over time.
Intercostal	The set of muscles between the ribs.
Introns	Non-coding DNA within a gene. Introns must be removed before translation. See also **exons**.
Lipase	An enzyme produced by the pancreas that catalyses the breakdown of fats.
Lipids	Fats made up of molecules containing the elements carbon, hydrogen and oxygen. Triglycerides and phospholipids are two groups of lipid.
Locus	The position of a gene on a chromosome (plural = loci).

Mass flow	The movement of large volumes of fluid within tubes. An efficient transport system for large organisms.
Meiosis	Cell division that shuffles the genes on the chromosomes so that no two gametes are the same. One diploid cell gives rise to four haploid cells.
Mesophyll	Cells inside a leaf, located between the upper and lower epidermis. The cells have a large surface area in contact with the air spaces around them.
Messenger RNA (mRNA)	A single strand of nucleotides that is made on a gene during transcription. Basically, it is a mobile copy of a gene.
Metabolic rate	The rate of metabolism, which is basically the same as the rate of respiration. Measured in oxygen consumption/heat production, per unit of mass per unit of time.
Micelles	Tiny droplet spheres that are formed when lipids mix with water, with the hydrophilic heads facing the water and the hydrophobic tails facing each other. The droplets have a large surface area.
Microorganism	Any organism too small to see with the naked eye. Applies to bacteria, algae, yeast and various protoctists such as amoeba.
Mitosis	Standard cell division. One diploid cell gives rise to two identical diploid cells.
Monoculture	Agricultural practice of growing just one crop, often in large fields created by removing hedgerows. Makes economic sense but reduces biodiversity.
Monosaccharide	Single sugar. Common examples include glucose, fructose and galactose.
Multiple repeats	Repeated sequences of DNA found in non-coding regions of genome, between genes. Forms the basis for genetic profiling.
Mutagen	An environmental factor that causes mutation, such as ionising radiation, ultraviolet light and chemicals such as mustard gas and cigarette smoke.
Mutation	A change in an organism's DNA. Gene mutations are changes in the base sequence of a particular gene, while chromosome mutations involve changes in whole blocks of genes.
Mutation	A change in the genetic material of an organism. A gene mutation is a change in the base sequence of a gene, which will probably result in a change in the amino acid sequence. In turn, this may affect the overall shape and, therefore, the functioning of the protein. Mutation is the ultimate source of all variation.
Myocardium	Heart muscle.
Non-disjunction	A chromosome mutation that occurs during cell division in which one cell gets an extra chromosome, leaving another cell with one less than it should have.
Normal distribution	Pattern of distribution, which shows as a bell-shaped curve on a graph, in which most values fall in the middle, with fewer at the extremes.

Nucleic acid	Class of organic molecules that includes DNA and the various types of RNA. So called because they are weakly acidic and (originally thought to be) found in the nucleus. All contain nucleotides.
Nucleotide	Basic sub-unit of a nucleic acid, consisting of a sugar (deoxyribose or ribose), a phosphate and one of four bases.
Oxygen dissociation curve	Graph that shows the properties of haemoglobin. The x-axis shows the oxygen tension (basically; the amount of oxygen available) and the y-axis shows the % saturation of haemoglobin with oxygen. The further to the left the curve is, the greater the affinity of Hb for oxygen.
Pancreatic juice	Secreted by the pancreas; contains numerous amylase, protease and lipase enzymes.
Pepsin	An enzyme in gastric juices that breaks down proteins into polypeptides.
Peptide bond	Bond that joins two amino acids in a dipeptide.
Phenotype	The observable features of an organism (genotype + environment = phenotype). Compare with **genotype**.
Phenylketonuria (PKU)	A genetic disease in which a faulty allele fails to make the enzyme phenylalanine hydroxylase, so that the individual cannot convert phenylalanine to tyrosine. The result is a build-up of the phenylalanine which leads to brain damage.
Phloem	One of two main types of conducting tissue in plants (see **xylem**). Phloem carries the products of photosynthesis from where they are made ('sources', usually leaves or storage organs) to where they are needed ('sinks', such as growing points, flowers, fruits). This process is called **translocation**.
Phylogenetic	In taxonomy, from origin of phyla: what evolved from what? A phylogenetic tree shows evolutionary history.
Plasma	The fluid component of blood, not the cells.
Plasmid	Tiny circles of DNA found in the cytoplasm of bacteria. Contain useful rather than essential genes.
Polymer	Large organic molecule formed by combining many smaller molecules (monomers) in a regular pattern. Polysaccharides, proteins and nucleic acids are all polymers. In biology, polymers are made by condensation reactions and split by hydrolysis.
Polynucleotide	A polymer of nucleotides, for example, DNA and RNA.
Polypeptide	A chain of amino acids that will fold and bend into a particular shape. Proteins are made from one or more polypeptides.
Polysaccharide	Large carbohydrate molecule made from repeated monosaccharide units. Starch, glycogen and cellulose are all polymers of glucose.
Potometer	A device that measures transpiration (water loss) from a leafy shoot.

Precision	The closeness of repeated measurements to one another. Precision involves choosing the right apparatus and using it properly. Precise readings are not necessarily accurate (close to the true value). A faulty piece of equipment or incorrectly used apparatus may give very precise readings (all repeated values are close together) but inaccurate (not true) results. For example, in an experiment with a colorimeter, using a dirty or scratched cuvette (sample tube) might give precise readings, but they will be highly inaccurate.
Primary structure	In a protein, the sequence of amino acids. For example, val-his-leu-his-met.
Prokaryotic cell	Simple cells with no true nucleus or complex organelles. Bacteria are prokaryotic.
Protease	An enzyme that that catalyses the breakdown of protein.
Protein	Large molecules made from one or more polypeptides (polymers of amino acids). Of fundamental importance in living things.
Protein synthesis	Two-stage process. The first phase is transcription: the base sequence on a gene is copied to make a molecule of mRNA. The second phase is translation: the base sequence on the mRNA is used to assemble amino acids in the right order to make a polypeptide/protein.
Proteome	The complete set of proteins that are coded for in a cell.
Protoctist	One of the four eukaryote kingdoms (along with plants, animals and fungi). Contains algae (including seaweeds), sponges and various unicellular organisms such as amoeba and plasmodium (the malaria-causing organism).
Pulmonary circulation	The circulation through the lungs and back to the heart. Contrast with the systemic circulation, which carries blood around the rest of the body.
Purkinje fibres	Specialised cardiac muscle fibres that initiate contraction of the ventricles. This contraction begins at the apex so that blood is forced up into the arteries.
Purkyne fibres	Alternative spelling of Purkinje.
Quaternary structure	In a protein with more than one polypeptide, the overall shape of the molecule.
Radioactive tracer	A radioactive isotope which is tracked and detected by an external radiation detector.
Random fertilisation	The fact that any egg can be fertilised by any sperm. Another important source of variation, along with crossover and independent assortment.
Replicate	A repeat: An experiment that is repeated is a replicate experiment.
Respiration	Universal process in which energy is released from organic molecules such as glucose or lipid, and transferred to ATP so that the cell has instant energy.
Respiratory centre	Region in the medulla of the brain responsible for depth and frequency of breathing.
Ribosome	Organelle that is the site of **translation** in protein synthesis. In eukaryotic cells, found free in the cytoplasm or attached to rough endoplasmic reticulum.

RNA polymerase	Enzyme that catalyses the addition of complementary nucleotides during transcription. The first stage of protein synthesis where the messenger RNA (mRNA) is assembled on a gene.
Root pressure	One of the two forces that move water up a plant, the other being cohesion tension. Root pressure is more significant in small plants, but not powerful enough to force water up to the tops of trees.
Scientific name	Two-part name, usually from Latin or Greek, given to each species. For example, *Homo sapiens*. Should always be underlined or in italics.
Sink	In the mass flow model of translocation, sinks are the parts of the plant to which organic substances are moving. Sinks include roots, fruits, seeds and flowers. See also **Source**.
Sino-atrial node (SAN)	Pacemaker of the heart: a bundle of heart muscle fibres found on the wall of the right atrium that initiates the heartbeat. Modified by two nerves from the brain.
Source	In the mass flow model of translocation, the sources are the areas from which sucrose is moving – the photosynthesising parts of the plant. See also **Sink**.
Species evenness	One aspect of diversity (see also **Species richness**). Refers to relative numbers of individuals of the different species that are represented in an ecosystem.
Species richness	One aspect of diversity (see also **Species evenness**). Refers to the number of different species present in a particular habitat.
Specific name	Name of the species; second part of Latin name. No capital: *sapiens*.
Spiracle	In the gas exchange system of insects, the opening of a trachea, through which oxygen enters the body and carbon dioxide is expelled.
Stabilising selection	A type of natural selection in which selection pressure favours the mid-range of a phenotype, i.e. selects against extremes. For example, average-weight babies are more likely to survive than very large or very small babies.
Standard deviation	A measure of the spread of data about the mean.
Stomata	Pores, mainly found on the underside of a leaf. They allow gas exchange.
Substitution	Type of mutation in which a particular base is replaced by a different base. Also known as a point mutation. Changes one codon, and one amino acid, but still has the potential to change the whole protein. Contrast with **addition** and **deletion**.
Superbug	Media term for bacteria that are resistant to a variety of antibiotics.
System	Group of organs working together. For example, digestive system.
Systemic circulation	Circulation of blood around the rest of the body but not between the heart and the lungs. See also **pulmonary circulation**.
Systole	Phase of the cardiac cycle in which the heart muscle is contracted. Compare with **diastole**.

Taxonomy	The science of classification.
Tertiary structure	In a protein, the precise, overall, 3D shape of a polypeptide chain. Maintained by hydrogen bonds and sometimes disulfide bridges.
Thermoregulation	Temperature control. See **endotherm** and **ectotherm**.
Tidal volume	Volume of air breathed in/out at rest. Average value in an adult is 500 cm^3.
Tissue	A collection of similar specialised cells that work together. Four main tissues types in the human body are muscle, nerve, epithelia and connective tissue.
Tissue fluid	Fluid that surrounds and nourishes living cells. Formed by filtration of the plasma through the permeable capillary wall. Composition similar to plasma but without the larger proteins.
Trachea	A large, supported tube in the tracheal system of insects. Mammals also have a trachea (windpipe).
Tracheal system	The gas exchange system of an insect. Basically a system of branching tubes that takes air from the outside to individual cells in the insect's body.
Tracheoles	Tiny permeable tubes that allow gas exchange between air and individual cells in an insect's body. See also **spiracles**, **trachea**. Tracheoles are permeable, trachea are not.
Transcription	First stage (of two) in protein synthesis. The base sequence on a particular gene is copied onto a molecule of **messenger RNA (mRNA)**. Takes place in the nucleus.
Transfer RNA (tRNA)	A cloverleaf-shaped molecule formed from a single strand of nucleotides that has an anticodon on one end and an amino acid binding site at the other.
Translation	Second stage (of two) in protein synthesis. The base sequence on the messenger RNA (mRNA) molecule is used to assemble a protein. Takes place on **ribosomes**.
Translation	Using the gene copy made during transcription to assemble a protein. Takes place on a ribosome.
Translocation	Mass flow system in a vascular plant. Sucrose and other organic substances are transported around a plant from **source** to **sink**.
Transpiration	The loss of water (by evaporation) from the surface of a leaf. Most water is lost through stomata on the underside surface of leaves.
Transpiration stream	The flow of water and dissolved ions from the soil, through the plant and out into the atmosphere.
Triplet	Group of three bases. Used interchangeably with the word **codon**. A sequence of three bases (for example, AAT, CGC) that codes for a particular amino acid.
Triplet	In DNA, a group of three bases that codes for a particular amino acid. Also called a codon.

Vascular system	A transport system in which fluid is moved around the organism in a system of tubes. Also called a mass flow system.
Vascular tissue	Conducting tissue. In plants, xylem and phloem make up the vascular tissues. In animals, vascular tissue refers to blood vessels.
Ventilation rate	Volume of air breathed in/out in one minute. At rest tidal volume $\times$ number of breaths.
Water potential	A measure of the tendency of a cell or solution to gain water by osmosis. Always a negative scale. Pure water has a water potential of zero.
Xylem	Specialised conducting (= vascular) tissue in plants. Consists of dead hollow cells with strong walls made from lignin and cellulose. Function is to transport water and dissolved minerals from roots to leaves – the transpiration stream.

Index

Notes

Notes